...iam Cecill, knight, Baron of Burghleigh Lorde high Treasoror of Englande

TR ab e ba
bj

1st Edn.,
1953

£6

Essex Yesterdays

The Common Seal of Colchester

Holidays into History

ESSEX YESTERDAYS

GEORGE CAUNT
OBE.

*To fellow historians,
particularly in the
Friends of Historic Essex*

Designed by Peter Tucker, typset in Bembo
by Kylin Typesetting and printed at
The Alden Press of Oxford
All Rights Reserved

The Kylin Press, Waddesdon, Buckinghamshire
© The Kylin Press, 1983
ISBN 0 907128 03 3

Contents

Introduction 1
Harwich: ALMOST THE STORY OF ENGLAND 2
Greensted: THE OLDEST TIMBER CHURCH IN ENGLAND 6
Thaxted: A PLACE TO DREAM 9
John Ray: SCIENTIFIC PIONEER 14
The Devil: AT DANBURY 18
Audley End: A STATELY MANSION 21
The Hedinghams 26
Edward De Vere: EARL OF MYSTERY 30
Chelmsford: EARLY INDUSTRY 32
Dick Turpin: AND THE HARVEYS OF HEMPSTEAD 38
Seaborne Raiders: THE BATTLE OF MALDON 43
Waltham Abbey: A MIRACLE 49
Borley: THE MOST HAUNTED VILLAGE 51
The round church: AT LITTLE MAPLESTEAD 53
Gestingthorpe: HOME OF CAPTAIN OATES 56
Finchingfield: KEMPE'S VOW OF SILENCE 60
Colchester: THE OLDEST CITY IN BRITAIN 63
Ancient Rochford: AND ASHINGDON 66
John Locke: A GREAT ENGLISHMAN 70
Pleshey: TOWN OF EARTHWORKS 73
Dedham: FAMOUS ARTISTS 78

The Tudor Palace: AT BOREHAM 81
Charles Dickens: AT CHIGWELL 84
The Rodings: AND JOHN THURLOE 86
Ongar: A MOST PLEASANT WALK 89
Clavering: THE MOAT HOUSE MURDER 94
Billericay: ONCE THE CAPITAL OF ESSEX 96
The Riches: OF FELSTED 99
Braintree: AND BOCKING 102
Tilty Abbey: AND THE HEADLESS MONK 106
The Saffron Crocus: OF WALDEN 109
Robert Fitzwalter: AND THE DUNMOW FLITCH 112
The Epping Hunt: IN THE ROYAL FOREST 117
List of Subscribers 120

Introduction

THE reader must have perceived that with me Essex is a passion, almost a religion. Sometimes in the London Streets, especially during long summer days, the thought comes over me of churches, inns, or clustered villages that I know, how they stand quietly through the hours, the sunlight travels round them and fades, and all the time perhaps there is no one there who appreciates their beauty as I do – at least, I am not there. This thought brings a strange mixture of exaltation and despondency. When my desire is fulfilled and I am bodily amidst the scenes I love, all else seems vain. I feel that I have come home; and I ask myself why have I been away so long? So much time seems to have been wasted. The curious thing is, that there is no disillusion; everything seems more beautiful than I remembered or imagined it.

Reginald A Beckett

Harwich

◆

ALMOST THE STORY OF ENGLAND

THE STORY OF HARWICH is almost the story of England. It has always been linked with great events from the earliest times.

When King Alfred was fighting the Danes, he sent a naval force against them at Harwich. This naval battle is described very briefly in the Anglo-Saxon Chronicle:

A.D. 885. And the same year Alfred sent a naval force into East Anglia. As soon as they came to the mouth of the Stour, then they met sixteen ships of pirates and fought against them and captured all the ships and slew the crews.

In 1326 Edward II's Queen Isabella landed with an army at Harwich and after a victorious march on London, deposed the King. Edward III started out from Harwich in 1338 with 200 large ships to invade France.

The great navigator of Elizabethan times, Sir Martin Frobisher, sailed from the Thames on 7th June, 1576, in an attempt to discover the North West Passage to India. He sailed up the North Sea and reached Greenland on 11th July.

He was back in Harwich in October with a captive Eskimo and a canoe. Frobisher on his third attempt to reach the North West Passage, sailed from Harwich on 31st May, 1578. This time he led a fleet of 15 vessels. He reached Greenland again and called it West England.

The last cliff he saw when he was sailing past he called Charing Cross! Frobisher thought he had reached Asia, and returned with a cargo of gold ore, which turned out to be a very poor stuff.

After a spell of unpopularity Frobisher was soon back in favour and was in command of the Triumph in the naval battle with the Spanish Armada in 1588.

Essex Record Office

On Friday, 5th August 1763, the famous Dr. Samuel Johnson set out by stage coach from London to Harwich to see off his friend Boswell, who was going to Holland. They travelled with a young Dutchman and a fat elderly gentlewoman.

What Johnson thought of Ilford is not recorded, but they stopped for lunch at an unnamed place. The woman chatted away merrily that she had taught her children

Harwich from over the cliffs

not to be idle. Dr. Johnson crushed her with the observation that he had been idle all his life and so had his friend, Boswell.

As the coach swayed along, she once again opened the conversation by saying how terrible the Spanish Inquisition had been, whereupon Johnson crushed her again by saying that only those who had attacked the established religion were punished.

After these verbal thunderbolts, he settled down to reading a book until the coach arrived at Colchester, where they stayed the night. The Dutchman engaged Johnson in a discussion on how much better the law was in England than in Holland. Johnson was not having this, and defended Dutch law to the discomfiture of the Dutchman.

Boswell had already earned the Doctor's disapproval by tipping the coachman 1/-, when the other passengers only gave 6d., as Johnson maintained that this excessive tip would make the coachman dissatisfied with the other passengers.

After a walk round Harwich, Johnson saw his friend off to his boat, but not until after Boswell had been crushed again by the Doctor. Venturing to maintain that the philosopher Berkeley's argument that matter did not exist could not be refuted Johnson said *'I refute it thus,'* and kicked a large stone so hard that his foot bounced back.

A famous visitor to Harwich in 1801 was Admiral Nelson. It was believed that the French might try to land near Harwich, and Nelson came to organise the sea defences. Although he was in the frigate Medusa, with a draft of 15-16 feet he was in trouble in the shallow water, and an easterly wind made it difficult for the Medusa to move; in fact the pilots refused to handle her.

In the words of Nelson: *'We have got the Medusa into this hole, but cannot get her out again.'*

But Nelson persuaded a marine surveyor, Mr. Spence, to help him, and they got the Medusa through a passage considered by the pilots too shallow for a ship of her size. This passage became known as the Medusa Channel.

In recent years Harwich became a fortress town during both World Wars, and during the second war had 1,200 air raid warnings and 1,750 bombs were dropped on this front line town.

Greensted

THE OLDEST TIMBER CHURCH IN ENGLAND

Coming into Ongar along the road from Abridge, a road turns left to Greensted Church, which is the oldest timber church in Essex.

When the bones of St. Edmund, King and Martyr, were carried back to Bury St. Edmunds in 1013, they rested at a small wooden chapel near Ongar. This wooden chapel still stands and, apart from certain alterations and repairs, remains much the same as it was 970 years ago.

The walls of the nave are built of the upright trunks of trees. Oaks were felled, split in half and morticed together, and the marks of the Saxon woodsmen can still be seen on the logs inside the church.

It was in the year 866 that a great host of Danes landed in Eastern England. They ravaged the countryside, burning, robbing and killing, and in 870 entered Suffolk. King Edmund of East Anglia gathered together what men he could but was defeated and captured by the Danes under their leader Inguar.

A description of the King's martyrdom was told years later to King Atheistan by a very old man who had been Edmund's armour bearer.

Edmund refused to abandon his Christian faith and curse God. Inguar ordered him to be bound tightly with sharp thongs. He was tied to a tree, and mercilessly lashed with long whips.

> 'But he continued with tearful accents to call upon Christ, and was not overcome. This exasperated his foes to madness; as if shooting at a target for amusement they riddled his whole body with the points of their arrows, inflicting wound after wound and flinging dart after dart.'

Greensted Church

So many arrows had been shot into his body, that he resembled a hedgehog. Still he would not yield, and the Danish leader ordered the executioner to cut off the King's head, which he did with a sword. As a final gesture of hatred, the Danes carried away the head and cast it into a thicket of thorns.

When the Danes departed from the scene of the murder, the surviving Saxons emerged from hiding, and found the headless body of their king. Search parties went out to recover the head, but without success until the head was found, guarded by a wolf, which was calling from a dense thicket *'Here! Here!* (or so it is said).

After some years the body of St. Edmund was enshrined at Bedericsworth which was afterwards known as Bury St. Edmunds.

When another invasion of Danes occurred in 1010, the remains of the saint were carried off to the walled city of London, for safety. The pagan Danish King Sweyn was warned by a monk, as the spokesman of St. Edmund, that the vengeance of Heaven would fall upon him if he did not mend his ways.

Sweyn roared like a lion and ordered the monk from his presence. But later in the day Sweyn was seized by a painful convulsion and died. It is written '*His son Canute who witnessed his fate, treated St. Edmund in after times with more civility.*'

So the remains of St. Edmund were sent back from London to Bury in 1013, and remained for one night at Greensted Church, which still survives, while only a fragment of the great abbey of Bury St. Edmunds remains.

In 1848 the lower ends of the oak trees, forming the walls of the church, were so decayed that they were cut off and replaced by a brick sill.

While the ancient timbers lay on the ground during the restoration, a great oak tree at Hoxne in Suffolk, which was traditionally the tree to which Edmund had been bound, was shattered by lightning. An arrow head was found embedded in the tree which by its position would have been there for 1000 years.

Thaxted

A PLACE TO DREAM

MAJESTIC giant! lordly Spire!
What joys thy aspect doth inspire,
When absent long from home and thee,
Thy towering beacon first I see!

Thy glittering vane (seen many a mile),
Proclaims my welcome with a smile;
And tells of home and evening fire,
Not far from thee, dear Thaxted Spire!

On Sabbath morn thou greet'st mine eyes,
I see thee ' pointing to the skies ! '
And thoughts of heaven my breast inspire,
Aided by thee, thou sacred Spire!

What lovely views of fairyland
Thy lofty summit can command;
All that a poet could desire,
Meets thy far ken, proud Thaxted Spire!

And I would wish, whene'er I die,
Beneath thy shade in peace to lie,
And greet, when human joys expire
Thine hallow'd precincts—Thaxted Spire!

                J. T., *Essex Literary Journal*.

THAXTED Church has been described as *'the cathedral of Essex,'* and its spire can be seen to perfection on the road from Great Dumow to Thaxted.

In the Market Street is the Guildhall, which is over 500-years-old, and we can stand in its shadow on a sunny day to admire the old houses of Thaxted.

The Church of St. John the Baptist is 183 feet long and the spire 181 feet high. Parts of the church date from 1340 and fortunately restorations have preserved the austere and cold beauty of the loveliest church in Essex.

The Civil War troubles arrived in 1647, when there was a *'Great Fight in the Church,'* and *'men and women in this fight fell all together by the ears, on the Lord's day,'* to quote the description of an eye witness.

'Mr. Hall, a godly learned Minister' was appointed vicar, but Lady Maynard nominated Mr. Croxon, who was described as a swearer and drunkard without parallel in the county of Essex. The two factions fell on each other in the church and belaboured each other with great enthusiasm.

As a result of the riot the Town Clerk of Thaxted was committed to the Fleet Prison in London, and the Mayor was summoned to appear before the House of Lords, who took a very poor view of the whole affair.

In 1910 the Rev. Conrad Noel was inducted as vicar. Noel was a well known Christian Socialist, and an anti-Socialist faction threatened to stone the Bishop of St. Albans if he inducted the new vicar.

There were disputes about ritual and incense, but Noel had powerful friends to support him as H.G. Wells and Lady Warwick were neighbours; Gustav Holst, the famous composer, became his Master of Music and trained the choir; and G.K. Chesterton and many other gifted people were admirers of the 'Red' Vicar.

During the Music Festival organised by Gustav Holst in the church, he writes:

'We kept it up at Thaxted about 14 hours a day. The reason we didn't do more is that we were not capable mentally or physically of realising heaven any further.'

The next great fight started in Thaxted towards the end of the Kaiser's war, and became known as the Battle of the Flags.

Conrad Noel decided to hang beside the old national flag of St. George the Green Flag of the Sinn Feiners of Ireland and the Red Flag of Socialism. Parishioners protested without any result and then a group of Cambridge undergraduates invaded the church, tore down the flags and put a Union Jack up. Down came the Union Jack, up went the other flags and the Union Jack was burned.

The Reverend Conrad Noel/Essex Record Office

A new Union Jack was carried in parades up and down the centre of Thaxted. Events took a more serious turn on Empire Day. Thousands of demonstrators poured into Thaxted, including a group of ex-policemen who had lost their jobs in the police strike and were known as *'Lansbury's Lambs.'*

The ex-policemen seized a lorry load of stones, which had been brought in to stone the vicarage, and drove it away to a distant field.

Rival demonstrations went on for some time, and then died down for a short period, Conrad Noel was defeated, however, when the dispute was taken to the Ecclesiastical Court and he was told to take the flags down.

But time smoothed down the ruffled feathers of Conrad Noel's opponents, and he had very few enemies when he died in 1942 at the age of 73.

There never seems to be any reason to hurry through Thaxted and, whether on foot or in a car, it is a pleasant place to stop and dream. If the visit should be on Easter Monday or certain other days in the year, there is Morris dancing, which was restarted in Thaxted by the wife of its famous vicar, the Rev. Conrad Noel.

Thax

h Street

John Ray, MA, FRS, the devoted natural historian/Essex Record Office

John Ray

SCIENTIFIC PIONEER

ABOUT two miles south of Braintree is the village of Black Notley. The Norman church and 15th century hall make it worth a visit, but the village of Black Notley is known all over the world as the birthplace and home of John Ray.

John Ray was born in 1627, the son of a Black Notley blacksmith. He must have been an outstanding scholar at Braintree, as the Vicar of Braintree arranged for him at the age of 16 to be admitted to Trinity College, Cambridge.

At Trinity College John Ray was such an outstanding success that he was made a Fellow. He specialised in natural history and became one of Trinity's most famous scholars.

His reputation spread beyond England and as the years went by he was acknowledged as the greatest authority in the world on natural history.

Before John Ray there was no systematic study or classification, and he established natural history as a science in place of the most ridiculous superstitions.

Not only was he a great scientific pioneer who took the greatest trouble and pains to verify the smallest detail, but a classicist, and all his books were in Latin.

So industrious was he that nearly 30 books came from his pen. He was also fluent in Greek, Hebrew, French and Italian.

The first book he wrote was a collection of English proverbs, many of which had been gleaned from talk in the village of Black Notley.

His first venture into natural history was in a book called *Catalogues Cantabryiam*, which was a study of Cambridge plants based upon his own observations.

He was fascinated by the magnificence of wild flowers and his 'interest in botany became a passion.'

John Ray was happy to have such a devoted follower as Francis Willoughby, who studied under Ray at Cambridge.

Willoughby was a wealthy man and did everything he could to assist his master in his work.

As Ray was of Puritan views, he was in serious trouble when Charles the Second was restored to the throne.

On ground of conscience John Ray could not conform, and lost his Fellowship at Trinity College. From a position of academic security, the naturalist was plunged into poverty and insecurity.

He returned to Black Notley and during the remaining 43 years of his life he devoted all his time to his work on natural history.

Owing to the unfailing generosity of Willoughby, Ray was able to travel extensively in this country and abroad.

Travel was extremely arduous in the 17th century and particularly in getting to the remote places necessary to obtain specimens.

He stayed for a time with his young friend Francis Willoughby at Middleton Hall in Warwickshire, but Willoughby died suddenly in 1672.

Fortunately Willoughby left him an annuity, which ensured that the naturalist would never be destitute.

Retiring again to Black Notley, John Ray devoted himself to studying the flowers, birds, fish and insects of Essex.

Within a year he married a 20-year-old girl, Margaret Oakeley.

He was rather pessimistic about the consequences of a difference of over 20 years between the age of his wife and his own, but the marriage was a happy one and his children were delighted to assist their father in his work.

As John Ray's fame grew, so his correspondence increased and the village carrier always had a load of natural history specimens, which had been sent for opinion and classification.

In 1686 his *History of Plants* was published, and was immediately considered as the greatest work of its kind. For his tremendous scientific work all Ray received was £5.

Even when he grew old and ill, the villagers brought plants and insects to him for study, and the '*Great Mr. Ray*' continued with his work until the end of his life.

The tomb of John Ray, Black Notley

He claimed that in the neighbourhood of Black Notley he discovered 300 kinds of butterflies, and that by observation he was certain that there were nearly the same number of different kinds of beetles and flies.

The great naturalist died at the age of 78 in 1705, and was buried in Black Notley churchyard, where his grave may still be seen today.

The inscription is in Latin, and the following is an English rendering given in C. Henry Warren's *'Essex'* –

Here in this narrow tomb, this marble span,
Lies all that death could snatch from this great man;
His body moulders in its native clay,
White o'er wide worlds his works their beams display,
As bright and everlasting as this day.

The Devil

AT DANBURY

DANBURY is a village about five miles east of Chelmsford. Danbury church is nearly seven hundred years old, and there are a number of Tudor houses and the 16th century Griffin Inn.

There is a legend that the Devil paid a special visit to Danbury church. The story is in a notebook of the Duke of Monmouth.

During evenson on 24th May, 1402, a Grey Friar entered the church and behaved so outrageously that the whole congregation was terrified.

At the same time there was a great blast of wind to which was added thunder and lightning. So great was the shock that the roof of the church was blown off!

But the official record is that the church was struck by lightning in a tempest and destroyed.

Danbury church was particularly vulnerable as 350 years later, on 5th February, 1750, lightning set the spire on fire and the fire burnt downwards for twenty feet.

There are three old carved wooden effigies of knights in the church. Two have their hands on their swords, and the other is in prayer. It is believed that the body of one of these knights was accidentally exhumed on 16th October, 1779.

The lady of the manor, Mrs Frances Ffytche, died and a grave was dug near one of the wooden knights. A leaden coffin was uncovered, and the workmen sent for the parson. It was decided to open the coffin to see whether it contained the body of one of the knights.

Inside the lead coffin was a substantial elm coffin. This was opened and another shell was revealed. When the lid of the third coffin was lifted, it was found to contain a curious liquid resembling mushroom ketchup.

Wooden effigies of three knights, Danbury Church

Mr. T. White, who wrote the account, said he tasted the liquid, which reminded him of pickled Spanish olives! Feathers, flowers and herbs floated in the liquid and the body of the knight was well preserved.

After the body was inspected by the parishioners and other interested people, the inner shell and wooden coffin were refastened, and the head coffin soldered. The knight was returned to his grave.

It was suggested at the time that the Knights Templars were buried in an embalming pickle, and that the dead man of Danbury was one of these religious warriors. He was probably a member of the ancient Norman family of St. Clere.

Sir Humphrey Mildmay, a great philosopher of the table and bottle, lived at Danbury during the first half of the 17th century.

He seemed to have spent the greater part of his time eating and drinking, and occasionally, to use his own words, he: *'Kissed the wenches exceedingly.'*

During the Civil War between King and Parliament, he remained addicted to his *'ordinary trade of drinking.'*

Often quarrelling with his wife, he was too happy-go-lucky to keep his domestic battles up for long, and once she ended a quarrel by sending him *'two cold pies and a kind letter.'*

Audley End

A STATELY MANSION

THROUGHOUT the country there are various mansions which should afford us more interest than many others of the more stately homes of England. Such a place is Audley End which is on the road between Bishop's Stortford and Cambridge.

The first sight of Audley End from the road is unforgettable, as enormous green lawns, across which flows the River Cam, lead up to the mansion.

Thomas Howard, Earl of Suffolk

AUDLEY END

The glory of Audley End is the Great Hall, which is 65 feet long, 25 feet wide and 29 feet high, and has a magnificent oak screen at one end. The beauty and taste of three hundred years have gone into Audley End, and it was the equal to Hatfield House, Hampton Court or Knole.

When the thrifty Scot, James I, visited Audley End, he was horror struck at such extravagance and said to the owner, Thomas Howard, Earl of Suffolk, who was Lord Treasurer, *'It is too much for a king, but it might do very well for a Lord Treasurer.'*

It all began in 1538, when Henry VIII gave the Benedictine Abbey of Walden to Lord Chancellor Audley. After Lord Audley's death, it passed through Margaret, the only surviving daughter, to Thomas Howard, Duke of Norfolk.

Audley End remained with the Howards until the death of Henry Howard, tenth Earl of Suffolk, in 1745, when it passed to Sir John Griffin (first Baron Braybrooke) and subsequently to the Nevilles with whom it remained until 1948.

Thomas Howard, Duke of Norfolk, to whom the estate came after Thomas Audley, was involved in a conspiracy to marry Queen of Scots and place her on the throne. Convicted of treason he was beheaded on Tower Hill in 1572.

His eldest son, Thomas Howard, first Earl of Suffolk, and first Baron Howard de Walden, began to build the present Audley End in 1603. Suffolk became Lord Chamberlain to James I in 1603 and Lord Treasurer in 1614.

Four years later he was charged with embezzlement of public money and, with the Countess, was committed to the Tower. After nine days imprisonment they were released on promising to pay a fine of £30,000.

In 1666 Audley End was sold to Charles II £50,000 as a royal palace, but the more careful William III, Prince of Orange, returned Audley End to the Suffolks in 1701 on condition that the claim was relinquished for £20,000 still unpaid on the purchase price agreed with Charles II.

The Howards lost Audley End in 1747, when the Countess of Portsmouth, a descendant of the third earl, dispossessed the tenth earl's heir.

The Nevilles remained at Audley End until the last war. The seventh Lord Braybrooke died at the age of 86 in 1941. His younger son was killed in the same year, and the eighth Lord Braybrooke was killed in Tunisia in 1943.

overleaf: Audley End form the south, in 1808. Audley End has been in the guardianship of the nation since the 1950's, and is open to the public during the summer months

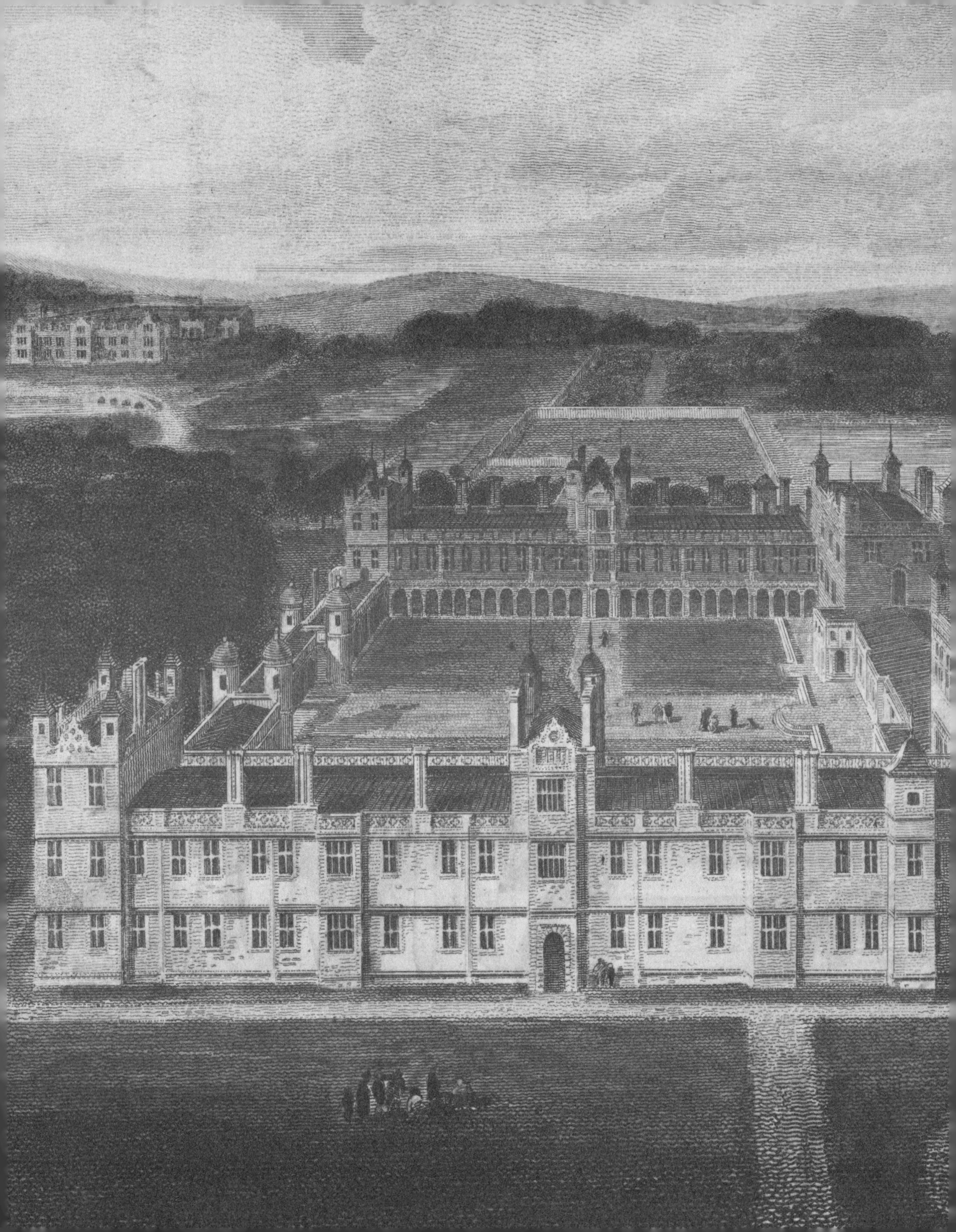

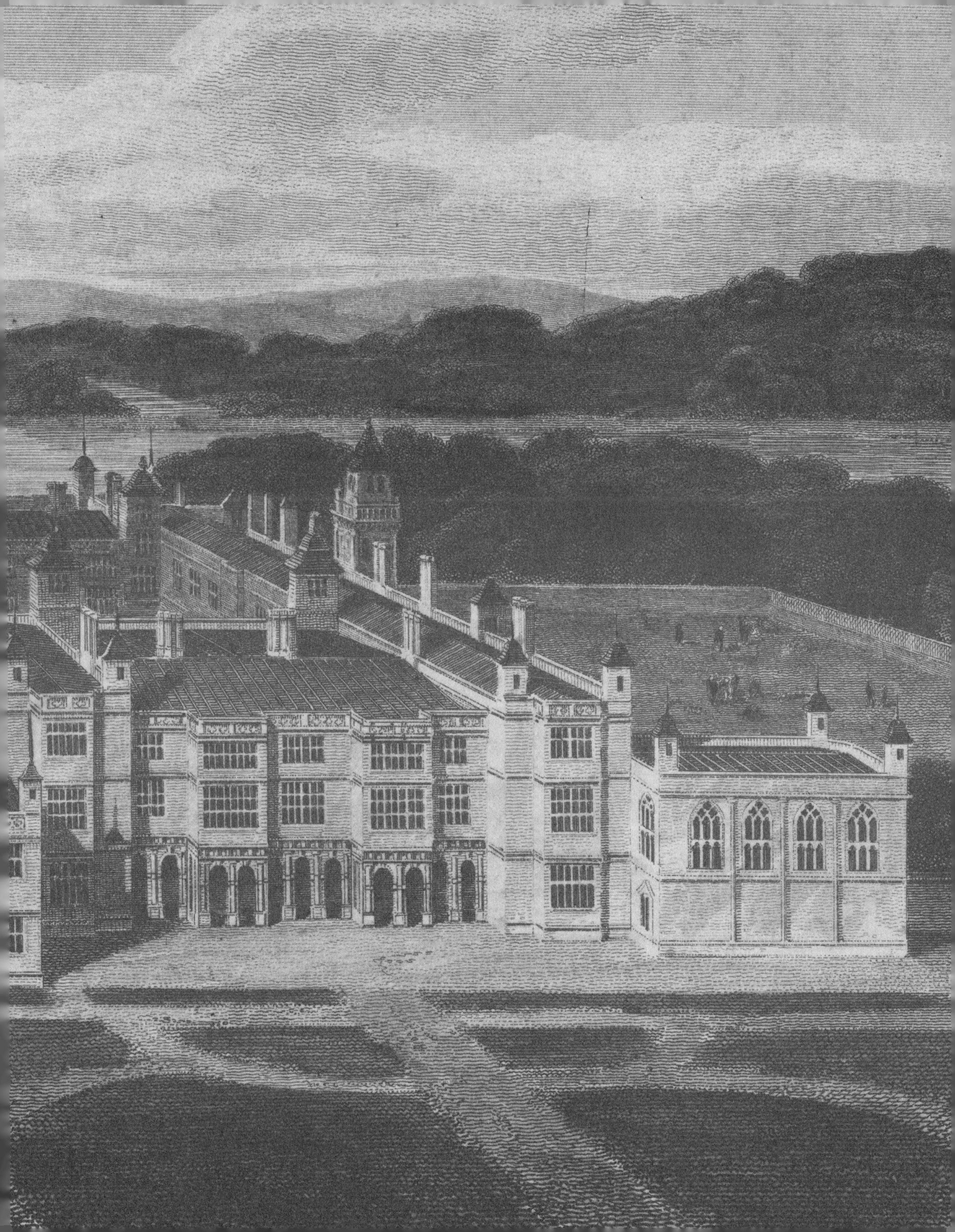

The Hedinghams

READERS of Conan Doyle's novels will remember *The White Company*, the story of a band of English mercenary soldiers who went to Italy in 1360 to fight in the Italian wars. The leader of the White Company, Sir John Hawkswood, lies buried in Sible Hedingham church.

He fought at Crecy and Poitiers, and then formed his famous White Company. Not only did he fight in wars, but deliberately caused them to give opportunities for employment.

At one time he fought against the Pope and at another time he fought for the Pope. He ended his life as the General of the Florentine army.

Witchcraft flourished in the remote parts of Essex, and as late as 1865 at Sible Hedingham a deaf and dumb old man of 80 was suspected of being a witch.

He was flung into a stream and pushed back again and again as he struggled to get out. Eventually escaping he staggered home and slept in his wet clothes. He was removed to the Infirmary, but soon died from shock and pneumonia.

Two of his tormentors were tried at Chelmsford Assizes for manslaughter and were sentenced to six months' hard labour.

From Sible Hedingham it is a mile to Castle Hedingham, and along the road the Castle (or rather the Norman Keep) can be seen to best advantage. It was one of the most formidable of Norman castles, as the Keep is 110 feet high and the walls 12 feet thick.

The Castle was built by the de Veres, described by Morant as *'one of the most ancient and illustrious (families) in the world.'*

The first de Vere came to England with William the Conqueror, and received as his reward 14 lordships in Essex. The second de Vere was made Lord Great Chamberlain by Henry I, and the third became Earl of Oxford.

The last Earl of Oxford (the twentieth) died in 1703 and the noble family of de Vere was gone forever. The de Veres were hereditary Lord High Chamberlains and also at various times Port-reve of London, Chief Justice, Chancellor, High Admiral, Lord High Steward and Constable of England. At the height of their power and wealth they owned the greater part of Essex.

The twelfth Earl of Oxford and his eldest son were on the Lancastrian side in the Wars of the Roses, and were both beheaded in 1461 by the Yorkist King Edward IV.

But the second son became the thirteenth Earl, and had his revenge against the Yorkist King Richard III at the Battle of Bosworth, when he fought on the side of Henry VII.

Henry VII was entertained royally by the thirteenth Earl at Castle Hedingham, but a little too royally, as the King fined him £10,000 for breaking the law which limited baronial power and pomp.

Financial ruin came to the de Veres with the seventeenth Earl, whose extravagance during the reign of Queen Elizabeth drove him to sell Castle Hedingham, which was purchased back by his widow.

Robert de Vere, the nineteenth Earl, was killed in battle at Maestricht in 1632,

The tomb of Thomas De Vere, Earl of Oxford

and Aubrey de Vere, the twentieth and last Earl died in Downing Street at the age of 78 in 1703, and was buried in Westminster Abbey.

The Lord Chief Justice of England, Sir Randolph Carew, in 1626, when the 19th earl succeeded, said:

> 'No King in Christendom had such a subject as Oxford... There must be an end... of names and dignities... and why not of de Vere? – for where is Bohun?, where is Mowbray?, where is Mortimer?, nay, what is more, and most of all, where is Plantagenet? They are entombed in the urns and sepulchres of mortality.
>
> 'And yet let the name and dignity of de Vere stand so long as it pleaseth God.'

The four daughters of John de Vere, the fifteenth Earl of Oxford

Edward De Vere

EARL OF MYSTERY

EDWARD DE VERE, the seventeenth Earl of Oxford, was born at Castle Hedingham in 1550, and succeeded his father when he was twelve. He was made a royal ward under the guardianship of William Cecil at Cecil House in the Strand. Edward was M.A. at fourteen and a half and was admitted to Gray's Inn in 1567 at the same time as Philip Sidney and John Manners, younger brother of the Duke of Rutland.

At nineteen the earl was rather short, with brown curly hair and hazel eyes. He was a great favourite of Queen Elizabeth, who called him her '*Turk*,' and would often send for him to go up-river to Richmond to dance with her and play the virginals. When the queen opened Parliament in 1571 Oxford attended her as Lord Great Chamberlain and bore her train from Westminster Abbey to the House of Lords. In the same year he was married to his guardian's daughter, Anne Cecil, in Westminster Abbey.

During 1575, while Oxford was travelling on the Continent in regal splendour and luxury, his wife gave birth to a daughter in England and he was overjoyed. On his return to England a scandalous rumour from the English court reached his ears that he was not the father of the girl borne to Anne. He quarrelled with his father-in-law, William Cecil, and refused to live with his wife. Oxford's resentment was further inflamed because his father-in-law was still able to control his purse-strings. A reconciliation came some years later and Anne bore him two more daughters.

Edward de Vere was a man of many skills. Besides distinguishing himself at tournaments in the tiltyard at Whitehall he was a poet of considerable distinction. In 1573 he published an anthology of poetry, *A Hundred Sundrie Flowers*, in which were included sixteen lyrics written by him, but they were published under pseudonyms, as it would have been an intolerable disgrace for a nobleman to have published his own poetry.

By 1579 Oxford was showing a great interest in the theatre, and in the following year took over Lord Warwick's company of actors. There is little doubt that Oxford wrote and produced plays with the queen's approval, but this was tactfully ignored, as such an activity on the part of a nobleman, particularly the premier earl, would have been a public scandal.

In 1586 Mary Queen of Scots was put on trial, and Oxford was one of the commission which tried her. From the next year he becomes a mystery man of the sixteenth century. He had lived a life of great extravagance and the vast estates of the de Veres had been sold. There have been a number of explanations of this sudden loss, and some have suggested that it was his father and others who had dissipated the great wealth of the Oxfords. On 26th June 1586, Queen Elizabeth, whose meanness was notorious, issued a warrant ordering the payment of £1,000 a year for life to the Earl of Oxford! In addition the parsimonious James I continued the allowance to Oxford until the earl's death.

The grant of £1,000 a year has been a puzzle which has never been solved. Was Oxford in charge of an Elizabethan M.I.5 ? Was Oxford responsible for political propaganda abroad ? Did Oxford receive the grant for providing theatrical entertainment for the Queen ?

When the Armada came in 1588 he fitted out a ship at his own expense and was in the running battle up the Channel. His wife died the same year, and three years later he married Elizabeth Trentham. On the death of Queen Elizabeth, Oxford bore the canopy over her coffin, and officiated as Lord Great Chamberlain at the coronation of King James I.

For the rest of his life he lived in mysterious obscurity at Hackney, where he died on 24th June 1604. He was buried at Hackney church, but his tomb has been lost.

It was not until 1918 that the claim was made that Edward de Vere was the author of the plays attributed to Shakespeare, and the 'Oxford theory' now has the support of many distinguished men who are neither cranks nor fools. There is a cautious comment in the *Complete Peerage*: '*In face of the prejudices of his day, which held literature and the drama Oxford's main interest to be beneath the dignity of a great noble, his work was mostly anonymous, or issued under the names of others. It is therefore impossible to assess his place in the world of letters.*'

But in the words of Shakespeare *Henry VI*, Part 3: '*O cheerful colours? see where Oxford comes?*'

The Shire Hall, Chelmsford in about 1830

Chelmsford

EARLY INDUSTRY

WHEN WE THINK of Chelmsford industry, the first name that comes to mind is Marconi. As early as 1897 Marconi opened a small factory to develop telegraphic communication without wires and today engineers come from all over the world to the Marconi College in Arbour Lane for training in wireless.

Romantic though the story of wireless may be, Chelmsford, or rather the nearby Writtle, possesses the distinction of being the first regular broadcasting station in Great Britain. Mr. P.P. Eckersley tells the story in his book *'The Power Behind the Microphone.'*

After cutting through miles of red tape and overcoming official obstacles, Writtle opened as a regular broadcasting station late in 1921 (the actual date is unknown) and was given permission to transmit once a week for half an hour.

The first programmes were records played on a gramophone which, of course, had to be wound up. I wonder if any of my readers remember the original call: *'Hullo C.Q. Hullo C.Q.'* (C.Q. were code letters meaning *'all those hearing me'*).

'This is two emma tock, Writtle calling.' (*'emma tock'* meant the call sign M.T.).

A microphone was held in the horn of the gramophone and, when the record was finished, the call was repeated:

'Hullo C.Q. Hullo C.Q. This is two emma tock, Writtle calling.' Then would follow an interval of three minutes before the next item on the programme was introduced, and concluded in the same way as before.

Writtle was soon giving live broadcasts with plays and famous singers.

overleaf: Chelmsford from Springfield Hills

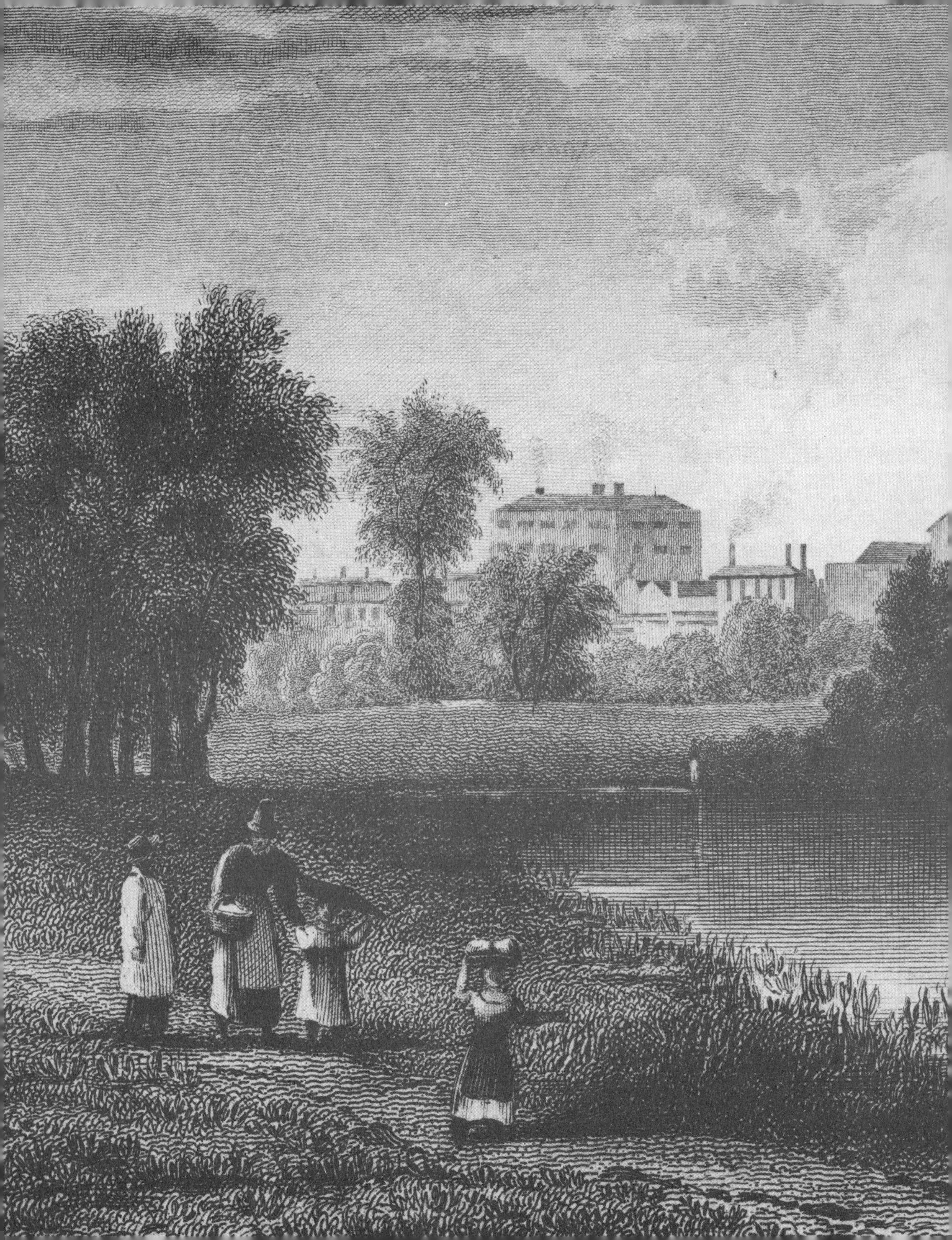

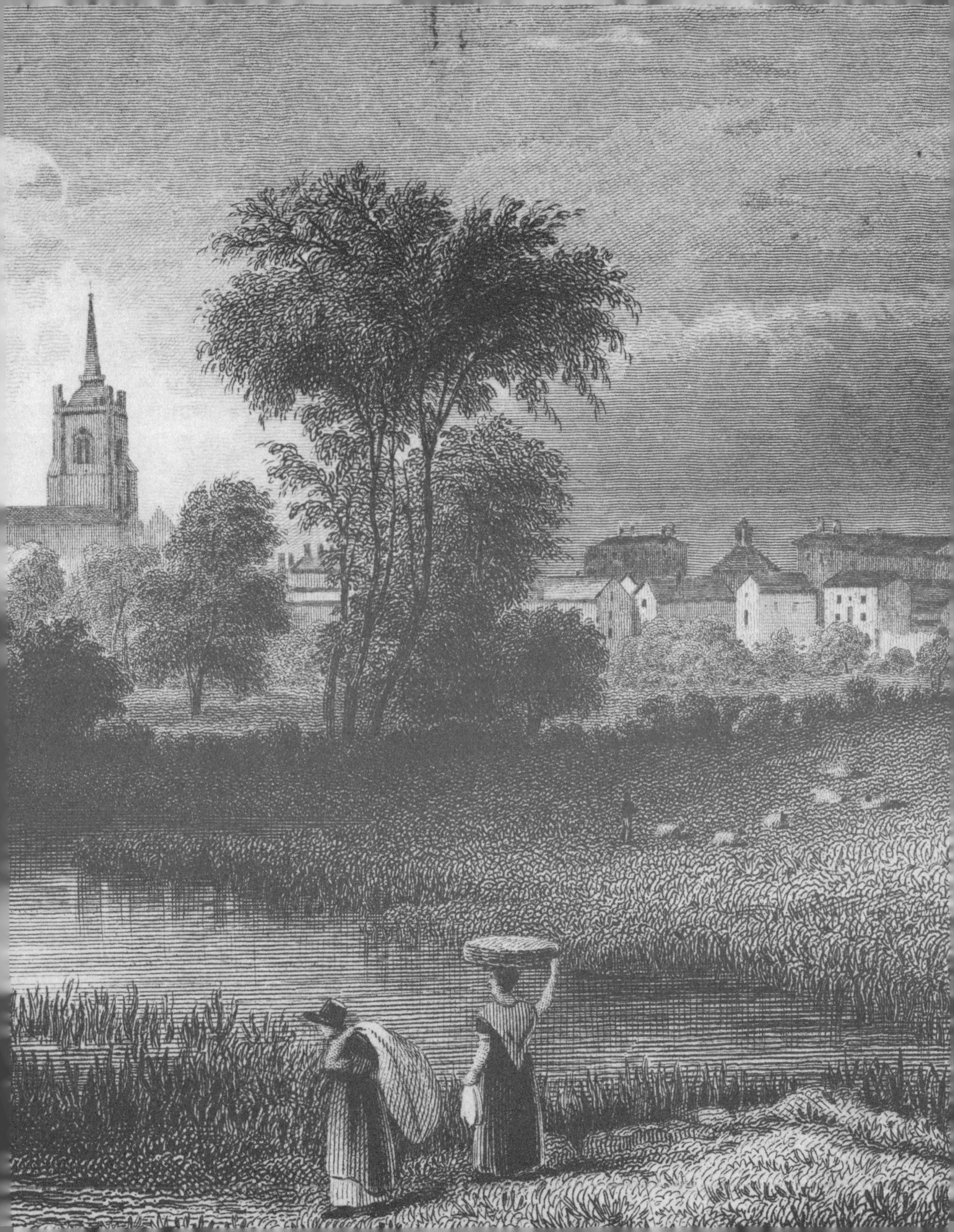

Celebrities were a problem in those days, as the Danish tenor, Melchior, was convinced that he had to sing into the microphone as loud as possible so that he could be heard in Denmark. The result was that his powerful voice shattered his microphone.

How frivolous and happy was wireless before the B.B.C. and Eckersley used to close the programmes by singing in a high tenor voice to the tune of Tosti's 'Goodbye'.

'Dearest, the concert's ended,
    sad wails the heterodyne.

You must soon switch off
    your valves, I must soon switch off mine.

Write back and say you heard me, your "hook-up"
    and where and how.

Quick ! for the engine's failing goodbye,
    you old low-brow !'

The B.B.C. was formed in November, 1922, and the first London station was 2 LO, which broadcast every day.

The B.B.C. started by being pompous and too serious, so Writtle started to take the mickey out of the B.B.C. and, what was more galling to the B.B.C., they were asked by listeners to close down on Tuesdays from 8 to 8.30, so that Writtle's skits on the B.B.C. could be heard without difficulty.

But Writtle soon closed down and in January, 1923, Mr. John Reith, General Manager of the B.B.C. appointed Mr. P.P. Eckersley to be Chief Engineer of the B.B.C.

Writtle was once honoured with a royal palace, as King John liked Writtle, and there is still a fish pond and a dried moat on the site of the palace.

Chelmsford church became a cathedral in 1914, and is a small cathedral for such as county as Essex, but although it cannot approach the nobility of Salisbury cathedral or even the beauty of the church of Thaxted or Saffron Walden, it has a small dignity of its own, standing serenely beside the busy Duke and High Streets.

South-east prospect of Chelmsford Church engraved by Mazell

Richard Turpin, executed at York in 1739/Essex Record Office

Dick Turpin

AND THE HARVEYS OF HEMPSTEAD

READERS interested in Essex will be well rewarded by a visit to Hempstead. This village is in a remote, north-west part of the county, five miles west of Saffron Walden.

Three men, whose names are world famous, are associated with Hempstead.

On the wall of the village inn, The Rose and Crown, there is a picture of a highwayman holding up a coach at a crossroad, with the words:

Dick Turpin's
Birth Place.

It is said that his father, John Turpin, kept the inn and that Dick was born there in 1705. There is an entry in the parish register of the baptism of Richardus Turpin. Although he was a savage ruffian, Dr. Johnson said of him: *'We have more respect for a man who robs boldly on the highway, than for a fellow who jumps out of a ditch and knocks you down behind your back.'*

In the church the Harvey Chapel is full of memorials to Harveys of the past, but the great William Harvey's bones lie in a simple marble sacophagus on which are the words:

THE
REMAINS OF WILLIAM HARVEY
DISCOVERER OF THE
CIRCULATION OF THE BLOOD
WERE REVERENTLY PLACED IN THIS
SARCO-PHAGUS BY
THE ROYAL COLLEGE OF PHYSICIANS OF LONDON
IN THE YEAR 1883

*William Harvey MD, physician to James I, later went on to discover the circulation of the blood/*Essex Record Office

William Harvey was born in 1578 and died in 1657. He gained his M.D. in 1602 and became physician to James I. In 1616, when lecturing to the College of Physicians he described accurately the structure of the heart and the circulation of the blood. His book, giving details of his discovery, was published in 1628.

He must have been a trusted friend of King Charles I, as he was given charge of the Prince of Wales and Duke of York at the Battle of Edgehill. While the battle was raging, he sat calmly behind a hedge with the two young princes reading a book.

William Harvey was a benefactor of the College of Physicians, as he supplied the money for the erection of a library in 1652. Owing to failing health he retired in 1656 and died in the following year.

The fellows of the College of Physicians followed his body to Hempstead, where it was laid in the family vault. In the presence of William Jenner, president of the Royal College of Physicians, in 1883, Harvey's remains were transferred to the marble sarcophagus, where they now lie.

Close by is the memorial to the other famous Harvey – Admiral Sir Eliab Harvey one of Nelson's bravest Captains.

Eliab Harvey was typical of his time. He lost £100,000 one evening gambling, and on a further hazard won it back!

Captain Harvey was appointed to the command of the *Fighting Temeraire* in 1803. In 1805 The *'Temeraire'* was off Cadiz with the British fleet.

When the French were attacked at Trafalgar, the British warships were divided into the Weather Column led by Vice-Admiral Lord Nelson, and the Lee Column led by Vice-Admiral Collingwood.

Nelson agreed that the *'Temeraire'* should lead the Weather Column instead of the *'Victory'* to mislead the French, but changed his mind, so he shouted through a megaphone. *'I'll thank you Captain Harvey to keep your proper station, which is astern the "Victory".'*

When Nelson lay dying, a French boarding party from the *'Redoubtable'* managed to get on the deck of the *'Victory,'* and the intervention of the *'Temeraire'* saved *'Victory.'*

Captain Harvey ranged his ship alongside the *'Redoubtable'* and the three ships were locked together. Then the *'Temeraire'* was attacked by the French ship

'*Fougeux,*' but a broadside from the '*Temeraire*' shattered the '*Fougeux,*' which was captured by a boarding party from the '*Temeraire.*'

Collingwood said of the action of the '*Temeraire*': '*I have no words in which I can sufficiently express my admiration of it.*'

Harvey was made rear-admiral, but four years later he was court-martialled and dismissed the service for violently expressing his disgust (in naval language) at the appointment of Lord Cochrane over him. Next year he was reinstated and advanced to vice-admiral and in 1819 to admiral.

So in this small Essex church two famous men from the same village and the same family lie close together – a great doctor and a great sailor.

'The Fighting Temeraire' by Turner

Seaborne Raiders

◆

THE BATTLE OF MALDON

MALDON is first mentioned in 912 in the *Anglo-Saxon Chronicle* and it was a borough by the time of *Domesday* book (1086).

There are many interesting old buildings in the town including the Moot Hall, which was built in the 15th century, three ancient churches, one of which was partly rebuilt to house the Plume Library, which contains a number of very rare books; the 15th century All Saints' vicarage and Beeleigh Abbey (¾ mile).

For hundreds of years Maldon has supplied warships for the navy. Two ships joined Edward 3rd's fleet for the siege of Calais in 1347 and a Maldon vessel was in the battle with the Spanish Armada. A long naval history can be taken as far as Dunkirk in 1940 when the small ships of Maldon helped with evacuation.

But the most famous day for Maldon, perhaps for Essex, was 11th August 991, when Ethelred the Unready was King of England.

A fleet of Danish and Norse raiders descended on England. They passed round the North of Scotland and down the east coast attacking Folkestone and Sandwich. After plundering Ipswich the Danes prepared to attack Maldon. One mile and a half down river from Maldon is Northey Island, which was selected by the Danes as a base for operations against Maldon, and the only way to the mainland was along a causeway (known as The Hard) which is covered with water at high tide.

The Earldorman or Earl of Essex, Brihtnoth, a brave old man decided that he would set an example to the rest of the country, and resist the Danes by force of arms. Hastily gathering together all available men he prepared to fight.

The story is told vividly by an unknown poet, who may have seen the battle, and

overleaf: Maldon

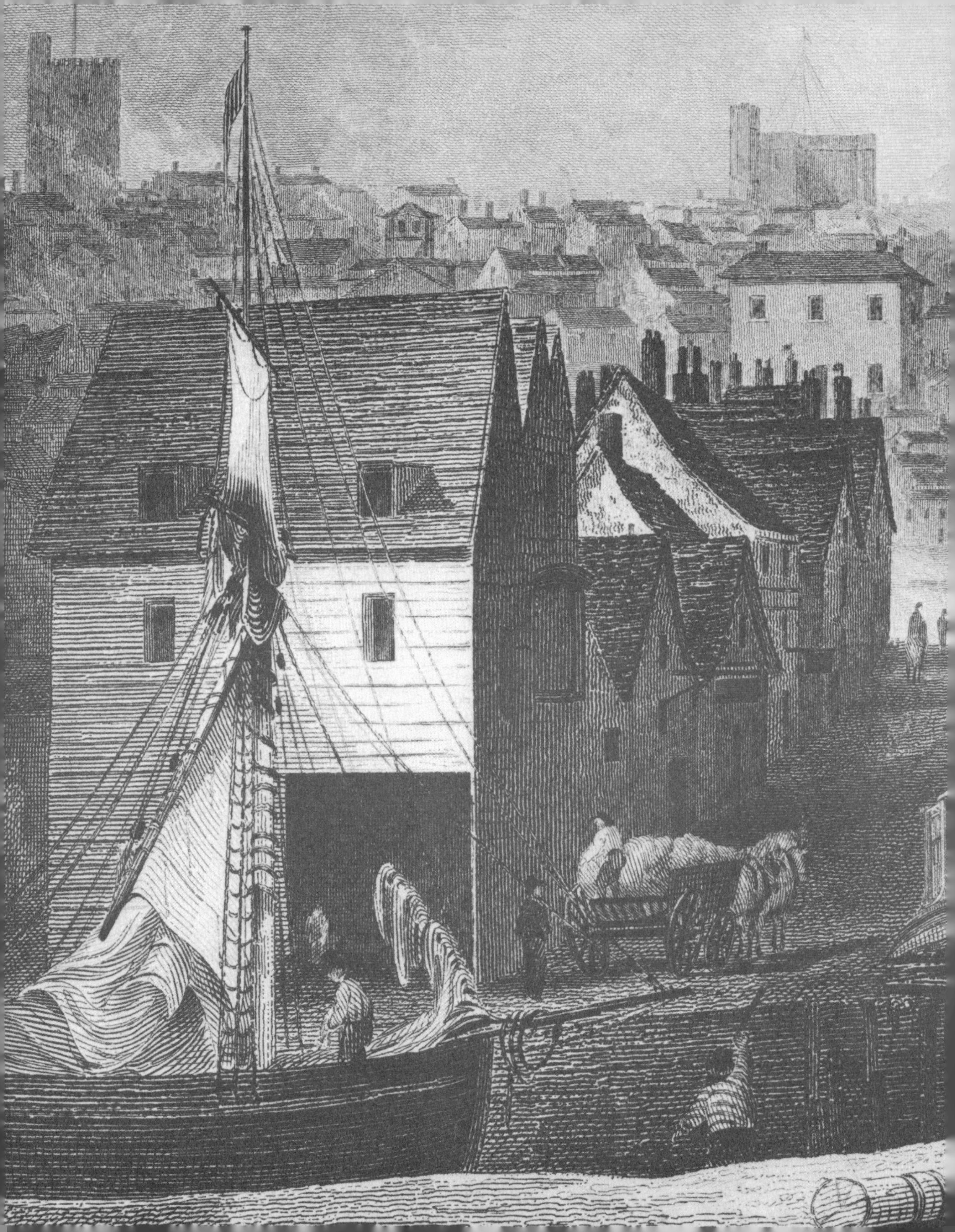

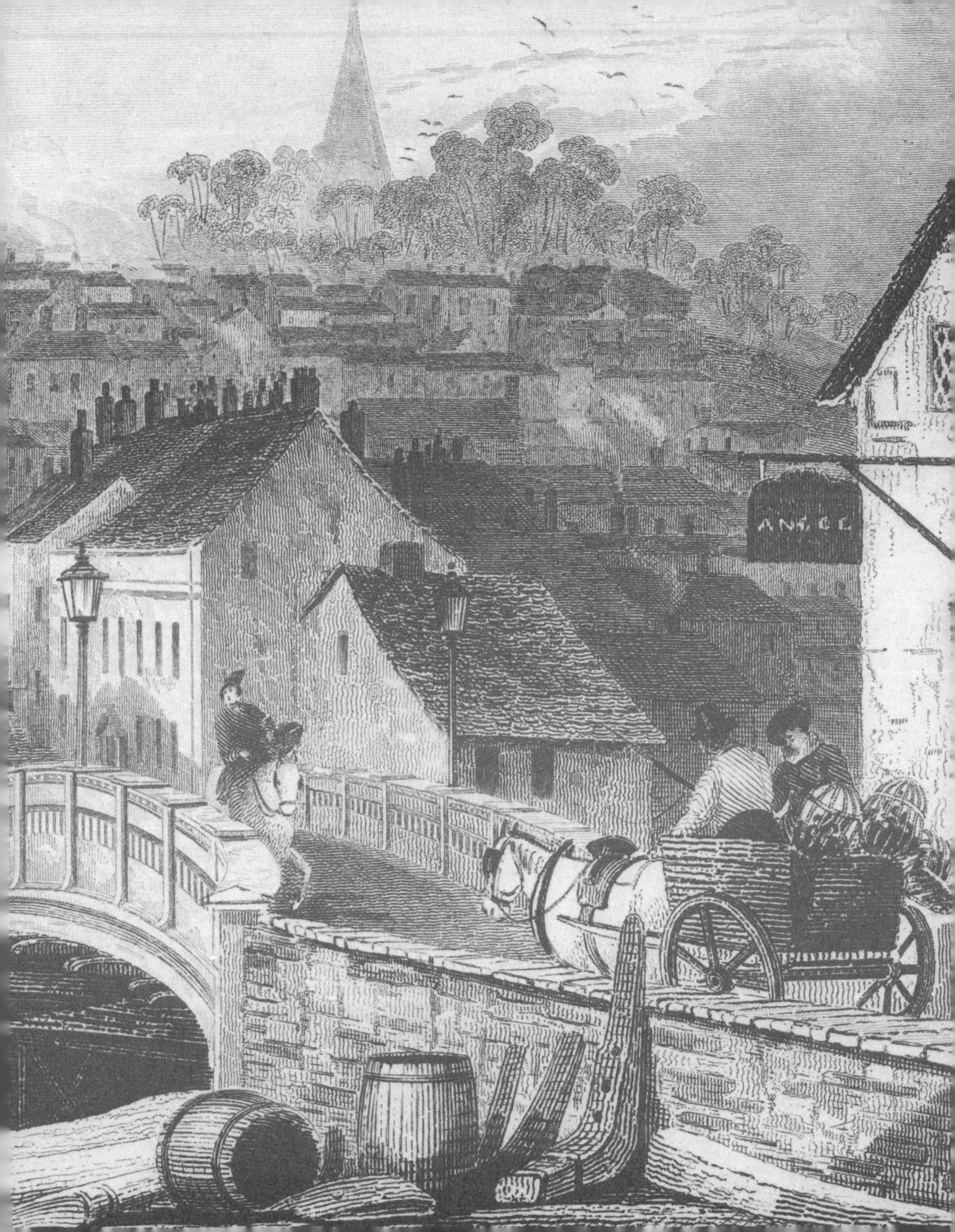

Saxon Ships, from an engraving in Strutt's Chronicle of England

a thousand years seems only yesterday as we follow the tragedy.

Some of the Saxon soldiers were youths who did not know how to hold their shields and weapons. Quickly they were shown how to stand and fight when the Danes charged.

One man who carried his hawk on his hand, released it:

*'He let then from his hands fly
The dear hawk to the wood and stepped forth to the fight.'*

The Danes were scornful when they saw the Saxon Army, and offered to depart if they were given gold and silver. Brihtnoth rejected the offer scornfully and said:

*'That here stands undaunted an earl with his army
Who will defend this country.'*

As the Saxons were on the mainland and the Danes on the Island of Northey, the Danes started to cross the causeway. Saxon warriors drove them back with flying arrows thrust of spear and cut of sword, so that the Danes were baffled.

But they appealed to Brihtnoth to let them come across, so that the two armies might face each other and fight man to man. Giving up the advantage of his position, the Earl agreed and the two armies met in battle.

> *'Bows were busy, the shield took the point*
> *Bitter was the onslaught, men fell*
> *On either hand; young men lay dead.'*

Brihtnoth was in the thick of the battle and was wounded again and again.

The Danes were fought to a standstill but when it was known that the Earl was fatally wounded, part of the Saxon army (suggested by some experts to have been of Danish descent and with a personal loyalty to Brihtnoth) mounted their horses and fled.

Those who remained swore that they would fight to the death, and the veteran Brihtwold declared that he was old and would stay to the end. As his strength weakened, so his courage grew greater.

And then the Saxons fought on until they were annihilated. The Danes lost many men and as a final act of vengeance cut off the head of Brihtnoth and took it away with them.

The Abbot and monks of Ely came to the place of slaughter, and recovered the headless body of the dead earl. The remains of Brihtnoth were finally buried in Ely Cathedral in 1154, and when the coffin was opened in 1796 it was confirmed that the head was missing and that the collarbone had been cut through, as if by the blow of a two handed sword or a battleaxe. The scene of the battle has been located at South House, near the causeway.

Follow the promenade downstream for about half a mile until the old sea wall is reached. Turn right along the sea wall (a rough walk along a high embankment) for three-quarters of a mile, when we are level with the causeway that links Northey Island with the mainland.

It was on this causeway that the Saxon champions fought the Danes who were on Northey Island.

It seems a sad place even in sunshine, and the memories of a battle which took place 1,000 years ago linger between the sea wall and a farm called South House. On those green fields Essex men died defending their country against a foreign invader.

Waltham Abbey

A MIRACLE

WALTHAM ABBEY owed its beginning to a miraculous happening. A blacksmith at Montacute over a thousand years ago had a dream that there was hidden treasure in a hill. He went with the priest and other villagers, where they discovered a black marble cross.

Tovi, the lord of the manor of Montacute and master of the house to King Canute, decided to seek divine guidance. The cross was placed in a cart, and various holy places were named, but the oxen refused to move. When Waltham, however, was mentioned, the oxen broke into a steady trot right across England to Essex.

The Church of the Holy Cross was built at Waltham to receive the cross, and it was this church that was rebuilt by Harold, and further extended by Henry II as part of his penance for the murder of Thomas Becket.

When Harold marched back from York to fight William of Normandy at

Hastings in 1066, he knelt in prayer before the Holy Cross in the Abbey, and the head of Christ on the Cross bent down as if in sorrow.

'Holy Cross' was the English battle-cry at Hastings. Edith Swan-neck set out from Waltham on the last sad journey to identify the body of the King among the heaps of dead, and was only able to do so by recognising marks on his mutilated body which only she knew.

It is generally believed that the body of Harold was entombed in the Church behind the high altar, and there is a record of a stone coffin being found whose lid was engraved "HIC IACET HAROLDUS INFELIX".

Many famous people have visited Waltham Abbey during the centuries, and George Fox, the founder of the Quakers, stirred up a riot in the town when he preached.

King Henry VIII was a frequent visitor, and an amusing story is told of a jest he played on the monks (strictly, canons), some of whom used to visit the nuns of Cheshunt. After a report that some monks were at the nunnery, deer nets were spread across the road, and the humiliated monks on their return were netted like a herd of deer.

There is another story that Henry visited the Abbey and was not recognised by the Abbot. As the King wolfed a magnificent supper, the Abbot lamented that his dyspepsia prevented him from enjoying his food and that he would give £100 for the appetite of his unknown guest.

Shortly afterwards the Abbot was kidnapped and kept in the Tower of London on a diet of bread and water for some days. A generous feast was then placed before him, which he enjoyed with great gusto. As he wiped his mouth and sighed with satisfaction, Henry walked in and demanded the £100.

The Kings and Abbots have departed from Waltham, and the glories of the Abbey have vanished, but Harold Godwinson, the last Saxon king, remains for ever in this corner of Essex.

The Battle of Hastings, from the Bayeux Tapestry

Borley

THE MOST HAUNTED VILLAGE

BORLEY is a sleepy little Essex village on the Northern border of Essex close to Suffolk. It is within sight of the two Suffolk towns of Lavenham and Sudbury.

The village of Borley was almost unknown until 1929, when a series of queer events made Borley Rectory world-famous. The Rectory became a Tom Tiddler's Ground for every kind of ghost or bogey. Even that fearsome and fatal monster of Essex known as the Black Hound of East Anglia was believed to have put in an appearance.

A summary of the principal phenomena includes ghosts of a nun, a parson, a headless man, a man wearing a bowler hat, galloping horses and a coach, a tall dark man, a girl in white (or blue) and an old man.

Then there were such things as ringing bells, organ music, bumps, knocks and bangs, heavy objects like bricks or candlesticks moving violently all over the place, footsteps, wall writing, lights in windows and unpleasant smells.

All the spooky manifestations went on from 1929 until 1939 when the Rectory was destroyed by fire, and even after the fire strange things happened in Borley.

The famous psychic investigator, Harry Price, conducted a lengthy investigation over the years, and the account of his investigations *'The Most Haunted House in England'* was published in 1940.

As a possible explanation for this ghostly upheaval various legends were discovered.

When the Peasants' Revolt swept across Eastern England in 1381, Simon of Sudbury, Archbishop of Canterbury, who had some connection with Borley, was beheaded on Tower Hill, and some thought that the headless ghost was the Archbishop himself.

Another legend was that 700 years ago a monk from Borley Monastery eloped with a nun from Bures Nunnery. The couple went off in a coach drawn by two horses, but were intercepted. The monk was either beheaded or hanged and the nun was walled up in the nunnery.

This legend was abandoned when it was discovered that there had never been a monastery at Borley and coaches had not been invented 700 years ago.

Two more ghosts were those of '*Old Amos,*' a gardener of 200 years ago, who had been a local character, and the screaming girl who, for some reason, fell to her death from an upper window.

Opinion however settled in favour of a young French Roman Catholic nun, Marie Lairre, who left her convent at Le Havre to become the wife of one of the noble family of the Waldegraves of Borley. What was supposed to have happened is not quite clear, but she was eventually strangled by her lover and buried on the site of the Rectory on 17th May, 1667.

Eye witnesses who saw the spectral coach described it as a large black coach drawn by two bay horses. Sometimes it was driven by a headless coachman and at others by two men in top hats. With old-fashioned headlamps alight, it would sweep through hedges across the lawn or farmyard and then disappear.

After the Rectory had been gutted by fire, an ancient human jawbone was discovered in 1943 and the fragment of a skull. These were assumed to have belonged to the nun, and were decently interred in Liston churchyard in 1945.

Harry Price died in 1948 and it was then that a number of people who had visited Borley Rectory with him accused him of fraud, as the possibility of a libel action had been removed.

A critical investigation of the evidence was given in '*The Haunting of Borley Rectory*' published in 1956. Charles Sutton, a Daily Mail reporter, made Harry Price turn out his pockets after a stone had been thrown downstairs, and several large stones were found. Lord Charles Hope mentioned that Harry Price was also accused of throwing half-a-brick as a ghostly manifestation. However, a recent book has indicated that while Price cannot be absolved from suspicions of fraud, he could not have been responsible for all the reported manifestations.

Moreover, there have been many reports of "happenings" since his death. So, be prepared if you are passing through the village after dark for a ghost coach with two bay horses and a headless coachman, and do not stop to speak to any shadowy characters who are gliding silently through the churchyard.

The round church

AT LITTLE MAPLESTEAD

Not two miles from Halstead on the road to Sudbury a turning to the left leads to the village of Little Maplestead. Here in the rich agricultural land of North Essex is one of the loveliest miniature churches in england – the Round Church.

There are only two other round churches surviving in England – at Cambridge and Northampton – as the Temple Church in London was destroyed during the last war.

They were similar in shape to the Church of the Holy Sepulchre in Jerusalem, and Little Maplestead Church was built about 1300 probably on the site of an earlier church. In 1185 the manor was given to the Knights of St. John of Jerusalem, known as the Knights Hospitallers, one of the great religious military orders of the Middle Ages. The other military religious order in this country was the Knights of the Temple, known as the Knights Templars.

After the crusaders had captured Jerusalem in 1099 a hospital and lodging were established for pilgrims to the Holy City, and the monks who managed the Hospital of St. John subsequently became the Hospitallers.

Their dress was black with an eight pointed white cross on the breast the same as St. John's Ambulance today. The Hospitallers followed an austere Christian life and served the poor and sick.

The Knights Templars were Christian soldiers who banded together to protect pilgrims to the Holy City from attacks by Turks and Arabs.

The Hospitallers also became a military order and, with the Templars, combined the religious life of the monk with the fighting life of the knight.

Both the Hospitallers and Templars of the Middle Ages, were in the Crusades and would always be found in the most dangerous parts of the battles against the

Knights Templar

Moslems. Both orders grew in power and wealth, and in the thirteenth century the Hospitallers possessed over 19,000 manors in Europe.

The Templars and Hospitallers were deadly rivals and, from all accounts hated the sight of each other.

When the forces of Christianity were driven out of Palestine, the Hospitallers settled on the island of Rhodes and were known as the Knights of Rhodes. From military knights they became naval knights ceaselessly attacking Turkish ships. They were regarded as pirates by the Turks. Driven from Rhodes, they became Knights of Malta, as the island of Malta was given to them in 1530.

The Templars grew even more powerful and wealthy than the Hospitallers. This became their undoing, as they were disliked by both church and state. Several times during the 13th century it was proposed to amalgamate the Templars with their rivals, the Hospitallers, but the Templars contemptuously refused.

In 1312 the king of France, Philip, forced the Pope, Clement V, to suppress the Templars, and this was done savagely and ruthlessly.

Under torture the leading Templars confessed to every kind of sin and wickedness, but afterwards withdrew their confessions and were burned at the stake still protesting their innocence.

King Edward II of England was unconvinced that the Templars were guilty of the crimes they were accused and took no action against them until he received orders from the Pope. Even so, the suppression of the Templars in this country was carried out without severe torture and burning at the stake.

The property of the Templars was handed over to the Hospitallers, who survived as a military religious order until Henry VIII dissolved the monasteries, when all the revenues belonging to the Hospitallers were transferred to the Crown. This was the end of the Knights of St. John at Little Maplestead, but their church remains much as it was when the Knights worshipped there, though there was an extensive restoration in 1851-57.

The English grand priory of the Knights of St. John was reestablished in 1831 – but was not recognised by the Roman Catholic Church – and was authorised by Royal Charter in 1888.

The English order today controls the St. John's Ambulance Brigade and Association and also an ophthalmic hospital in Jerusalem.

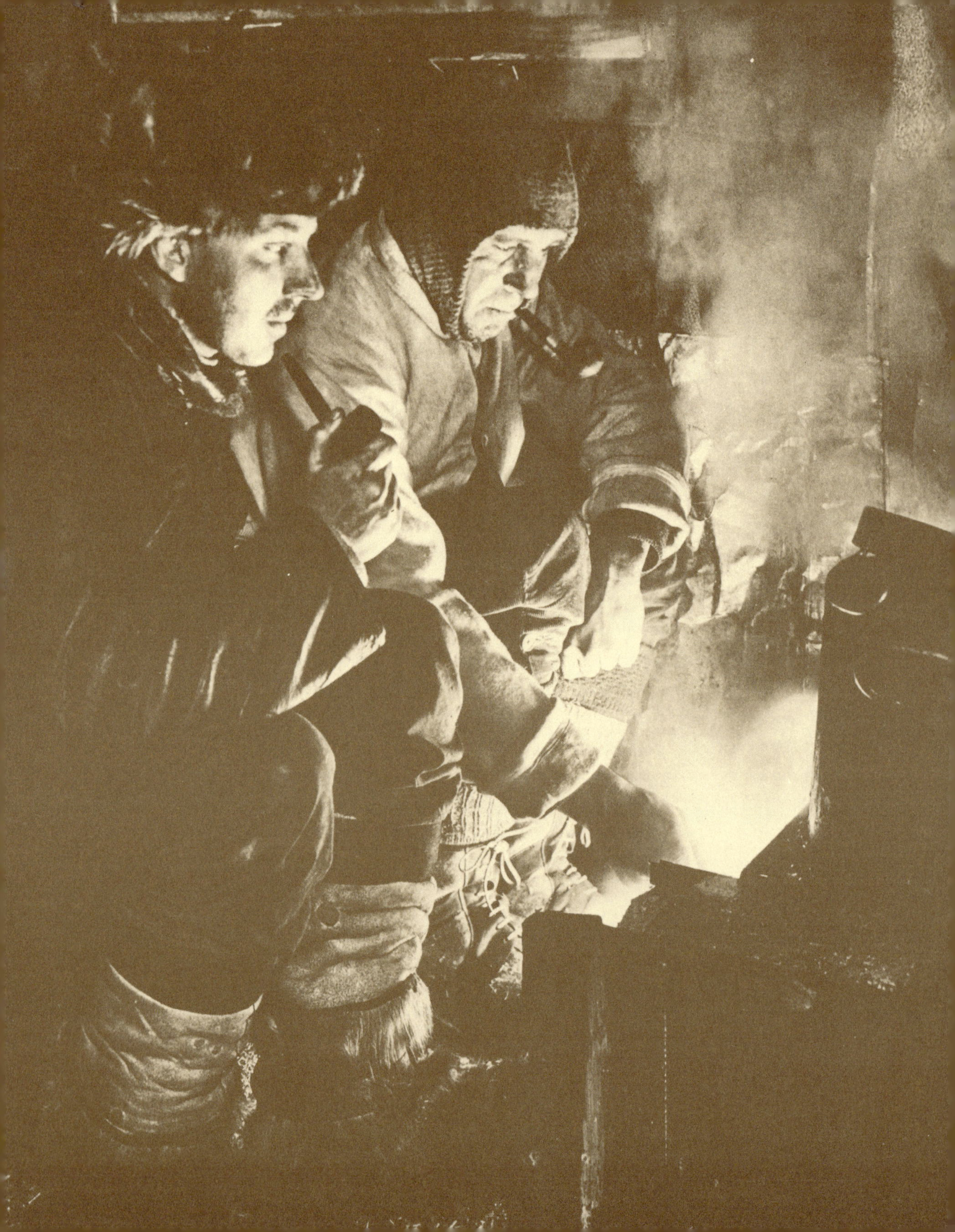

Gestingthorpe

◆

HOME OF CAPTAIN OATES

Near to Little Maplestead, Castle Hedingham and Halstead, is the curiously named village of Gestingthorpe, another of the unspoiled villages of north Essex.

The Tudor brick tower of the church is 64 ft high and can be seen long before the village is reached, and the hammerbeam roof of the church has been there for 500 years. The ancient beauty of the church is keeping with a simple brass tablet which tells briefly the story of a great English epic.

> IN MEMORY OF A VERY GALLANT GENTLEMAN,
> LAWRENCE EDWARD GRACE OATES,
> CAPTAIN IN THE INNISKILLING DRAGOONS,
> BORN 17th MARCH, 1880, DIED 17th MARCH, 1912
> ON THE RETURN JOURNEY FROM THE SOUTH POLE
> OF THE SCOTT ANTARCTIC EXPEDITION.
> WHEN ALL WERE BESET BY HARDSHIP, HE BEING GRAVELY
> INJURED WENT OUT INTO THE BLIZZARD TO DIE, IN THE
> HOPE THAT BY SO DOING HE MIGHT ENABLE HIS
> COMRADES TO REACH SAFETY.

And for many years the brass plate was kept clean by his mother, who used to walk to the church every week until she was nearly ninety.

Like most country boys of his time he grew up among dogs and horses, and it was his understanding of these animals which was the deciding qualification for him to join Scott's expedition.

opposite: Captain Oates (right)/ HG Ponting by courtesy of the National Portrait Gallery

At first Oates was a delicate boy, and he had to leave Eton after two years for health reasons, so his formal education was slight, but he was learning far more important things than he could have picked up at school.

Sea voyages and a busy life in the country transformed the delicate boy into a hardy young man as tough as nails and with an unbreakable will.

He was a natural soldier, and after two years in the West Yorkshire Militia he received a commission in the 6th Inniskilling Dragoons.

Oates arrived in South Africa in time to be on active service in the Boer war. He was leading a patrol which was attacked by Boers, and covered the retreat of his men until only he was left facing the enemy. A Boer bullet broke his thigh, and, in answer to appeals to surrender, replied that he was there to fight not surrender. Thus came his first nickname: *'No surrender Oates.'*

After recovering from his wound, he served in India, but found everything rather dull, and imported a pack of hounds to hunt hyenas.

Captain Scott was fitting out his Antarctic expedition, and Oates eagerly applied to go. When asked for his qualifications, he said that he understood dogs and horses, had a pack of hounds, and knew all about the use of Manchurian ponies in Tibet. Captain Scott selected him.

The preparations for the expedition were completed and in June 1910, the Terra Nova sailed for New Zealand. It took five months to reach New Zealand, during which time the members of the party prepared for the great adventure before them.

By December the Terra Nova was sailing among icebergs, and on Christmas Day they were icebound. Christmas dinner was a hilarious affair with Oates contributing a countryman's song to the entertainment – *'The Fly is on the Turnip.'*

Land was sighted on New Year's Day and soon all efforts were being directed to establishing a winter base. The dogs and ponies were frantic with joy at getting off the boat, and all settled down to wait for the Antarctic winter to pass.

It was the following November before a start could be made and the party of men and animals pushed on as speedily as they could in frightful conditions, struggling through a perpetual blizzard.

Captain Oates ultimately had to perform a heartrending task under these terrible conditions, and shoot the ponies.

When the first supply depot was established, the twelve explorers sent the dogs back and walked on with their laden sledges.

Four men were left behind as a support party, and the remaining eight struggled on through Christmas towards the Pole. One man was sent back through illness, and by January, 1912 they had reached their destination to find that the Norwegian expedition under Amundsen had reached the Pole before them and departed.

The English explorers had a celebration supper, but Scott wrote in his diary: *'Great God, this is an awful place.'*

Then came the nine hundred miles walk back. It was hopeless and death was inevitable. But the men struggled to reach their camp.

Oates realised that his death was near, and that he would only be a hindrance to his comrades. He expected to die in his sleep, and on his last night he talked of his mother in Gestingthorpe and the Essex farms and meadows.

With the last words – '*I am just going outside, and I may be some time,*' he stepped out into the blizzard and was never seen again.

His grave was the Antarctic. The search party recovered the bodies of the other men, but not Captain Oates. Near the place of his death, a wooden cross was put up, on which was carved:

Hereabouts died a man R.I.P.

Finchingfield

KEMPE'S VOW OF SILENCE

FINCHINGFIELD is the loveliest of Essex villages. Indeed, its only rivals – in my estimation – are in the Cotswolds. The village is in a backwater of Essex, although it is easily reached by car through Ongar, Great Dunmow and Great Bardfield.

There are so many charming corners of Finchingfield that I can only leave it to readers to pay a visit and see for themselves an Essex village at its best.

The most imposing spectacle at Finchingfield is undoubtedly the Elizabethan manor house, Spains Hall at which one of the strangest and most tragic series of events took place.

William Kempe, of Spains Hall, Finchingfield, was a typical hot-tempered man of the sixteenth century. Accusing his wife Philippa, of infidelity after 33 years of married life, the old man of 66 stormed out of Spains Hall and tramped through the woods of his estate tormented by his own black thoughts.

The memory of his wife's stricken face, and his recollection of so many previous occasions, when he had only wished that he could take back what he had said, decided him that he would be silent for the rest of his life. As he called on God as a witness to his oath of silence, a man emerged from the shadow of the trees.

'Raven' Foster, the seventh son of a seventh son, at whose birth three ravens had croaked through the night, warned William Kempe that his vow of silence would only bring on himself calamity and disaster. The 'Raven' implored him to take back the oath before it was too late, but the old man set his lips. There was no turning back.

A storm over the west front of Spains Hall

Next day, the Squire was dumb and at first it was thought that some strange malady had struck him. The parson and the doctor tried their best to break through the curtain of silence, but William Kempe would not say a word.

The only communication he would have with those about him was by written notes to indicate his wishes.

To mark the years of his silence he planned seven fish ponds. At the end of the first year, when the first pond was nearly completed, three of his servants were drowned in it in mysterious circumstances. The next year when the second pond was completed, his broken-hearted wife died.

The third year after the third pond was completed, Kempe was thrown from his horse while riding home at night. His leg was broken and he lay helpless through the night as his vow would not permit him to call for help. A long illness left him still with unbroken will.

The other tragic event of which there is record came at the end of the fifth year. Having gone out with his groom on business to another village he decided to return to Spains Hall the same night although a heavy storm was about to break.

The two men rode through the gathering darkness, but heavy rain drove them to shelter in the upper floor of a ruined castle.

As William Kempe sat moody and silent waiting for the storm to abate, he heard a gang of robbers in the room below planning an attack on Spains Hall. Signalling to his groom to follow him, the two men escaped from the ruin, and rode fast through the night to prepare the household to resist attack.

The River Blackwater was in flood and it was impossible for old William Kempe to cross. The groom was unaware of the conversation his master had overheard in the ruin, but from Kempe's desperate behaviour understood that there was frightful urgency.

Still refusing to speak, Kempe wrote a message for the groom to take across the river to Spains Hall, while he took the longer and easier route.

The groom managed to get his horse across the river and arrived safely at the Hall, but the message so carefully written was soaked with rain and unreadable. Not knowing what danger threatened, all the men decided to arm themselves and ride to meet William Kempe.

When the gang of thieves arrived at Spains Hall, it was unguarded and after murdering a young boy who was a relative of Kempe, they departed with everything they could lay their hands on.

William Kempe remained in his gloomy silent world until the end of 1625, when a new parson, Stephen Marshall, came to Finchingfield. Marshall was a Puritan and destined to become a famous churchman under Oliver Cromwell.

What happened between Kempe and Marshall is unknown, but early in 1626 William Kempe not only spoke again but took a prominent part in the affairs of the parish after nearly six years of silence. Hundreds of spectators gathered to see William Kempe attend public worship in the church.

But another silence was to come to Kempe two years later, when he had a stroke. As he lay speechless on his bed, his pathetic efforts to make his last wishes known failed, and he died with his will unmade on 10th June, at the age of 73.

He was buried beside his long-suffering wife in Finchingfield Church.

Colchester

THE OLDEST CITY IN BRITAIN

COLCHESTER city proud of its past and there is something in almost every street to remind the visitor that it is the oldest city in Britain.

When London was still a hill close to a swamp a King reigned at Colchester – or Camulodunum to the Romans and the name Colchester did not appear until long after the Romans had left Britain.

King Cunobelinus (5 B.C. to A.D. 43) reigned at Colchester, and it is believed that his tomb was discovered at Lexden, a suburb of Colchester, in 1924. He is better known to us as the Cymbeline of Shakespeare's play.

From the top of Colchester Town Hall a great bronze figure of St. Helena holding a cross dominates the city. She is the patron saint of Colchester and was the mother of Constantine the Great.

In the year A.D. 238, Coel was a Roman governor in Essex. He revolted and made himself King.

Old King Cole was a merry old soul,
*   And a merry old soul was he.*
He called for his pipe and he called for his bowl,
*   And he called for his fiddlers three.*

Helena was his daughter – a beautiful woman skilled in music and many other accomplishments. She captivated the Roman general Constantius who besieged Colchester and, according to the legend, Constantine was born before the marriage was solemnised.

Constantius became Caesar and his son, Constantine the Great, succeeded him.

Colchester Castle in about 1830

Helena was converted to Christianity by her son and became famous for her piety and charity. When some alterations were taking place at Jerusalem under her orders, three wooden crosses were found. The coat of arms of Colchester consists of three crowns and a cross.

Colchester's right to St. Helena is, however, doubtful, as historians insist that St. Helena, the mother of Constantine, was born in Bythnia and was not an Essex woman.

All that survives of Colchester Castle is the great Norman keep, which is larger than the White Tower in the Tower of London. Colchester Castle is now a museum, which possesses the best collection of Roman antiquities in Northern Europe.

A short distance from the castle is Holly Trees mansion, a museum of Essex bygones, in which are included a magnificent collection of tea caddy spoons. Across the road is an ancient church, All Saints, which has been transformed into a Natural History Museum.

Walking in the Castle Park I discovered the memorial which marks the spot where Sir Charles Lucas and Sir George Lisle were shot by order of Lord General Fairfax on the 28th August, 1648.

Though King Charles I was a prisoner, the Royalists made one last desperate bid and Colchester was captured by the Cavaliers on 12th June, 1648. Oliver Cromwell was engaged in defeating a Scottish invasion and Colchester was besieged by Fairfax. The siege lasted until 27th August, when the Royalists surrendered.

Lord Capel and the Earl of Norwich were sent to Windsor Castle for trial, but Sir Charles Lucas and Sir George Lisle were sentenced to death by court martial and shot immediately. Their bodies were taken to St. Giles Church for burial and after the Restoration a black marble stone was laid over the vault with the following inscription:

'Under this marble ly the bodies of the two most valiant captains, Sir Charles Lucas and Sir George Lisle, Knights, who for their eminent loyalty to their sovereign were on the 28th day of August, 1648, by the command of Sir Thomas Fairfax, the General of the Parliamentary army, in cold blood, barbarously murdered.'

Sir George Lisle

Sir Charles Lucas   *General Lord Fairfax*

Ancient Rochford

AND ASHINGDON

ALTHOUGH only three miles from Southend, Rochford, on the River Roach, remains a country town with a manor house (Rochford House) and has an unusually charming church – St. Andrew's.

St. Andrew's church is close to the railway station and has two half-timbered gables, which I have never seen in a church before, and a tall tower of red brick.

Close by the church is Rochford Hall, which was built about 1545, and is on the site of the earlier Rochford Hall of Sir Thomas Boleyn, the father of Anne Boleyn. There is a legend that Anne was born at Rochford Hall.

Sir Thomas's father had been Lord Mayor of London, and accumulated a fortune as a city merchant, so the Boleyns were representative of the new aristocracy of money, who were pushing aside the ancient aristocracy of Norman blood.

Henry VIII took a liking to Sir Thomas Boleyn and made him treasurer of the household. Soon he was Viscount Rochford, and a court faction began to hate the growing influence of the Boleyns.

In 1526 the King, who was 35, noticed Sir Thomas's younger daughter Anne, who was 19. Anne's elder sister, Mary, had been Henry's mistress, but Anne's ambition was higher. She would be Queen.

Royal marriages were usually for political and diplomatic purposes, and the King's infatuation for Anne was to have tremendous consequences in the struggle for power in Europe, and in the establishment of the Church of England.

It might well have been that England would have broken away from the Roman Catholic church in the next 50 years, but the refusal of the Pope to give Henry an

Henry VIII, friend of Sir Thomas Boleyn, Anne's father

annulment of his marriage to Katherine of Aragon brought the religious revolution in England to a head.

There was usually no difficulty in getting a royal annulment from the worldly Popes of the period, but in this particular case Clement VII was effectively under the thumb of Katherine's uncle the Emperor Charles V. whose troops had already let loose a storm of violence and destruction in Rome.

So it was that Henry's new archbishop of Canterbury, Thomas Cranmer, annulled the King's marriage to Katherine and married him to Anne in 1533. Anne's great disaster was that, like Katherine, she did not bear the King a son, and in three years she fell a victim to court intrigue.

Henry already had his eye on Jane Seymour, and welcomed the chance of getting rid of the unfortunate Anne.

A trumped-up charge of immorality sent Anne and five men (including her own brother) to the block. Anne was beheaded with a sword by the executioner to Calais, who was brought over to the Tower of London for the purpose.

There is a tradition that Anne's head was buried in the church at East Horndon not far from Brentwood.

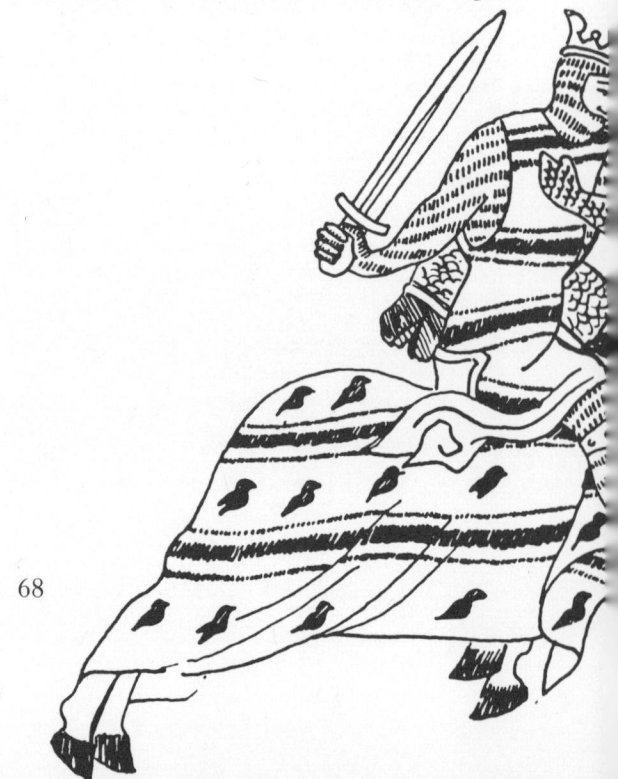

For hundreds of years Rochford had the curious custom of the Whispering Court, to which the lord of the manor summoned all his tenants to do homage to him. All proceedings were conducted in whispers and, if a tenant did not hear his name called, he was fined.

The Whispering Court continued until the last century, and became a great opportunity for festivities on Whit Monday. When the 'Court' was finished, a banquet of beef, cheese, pickles and beer was held at the local inn.

Two miles from Rochford on the Ashingdon/Battlesbridge road, a track to the right leads to Ashingdon Minster. The Minster is a small church, the tower of which has a curious pyramid roof.

King Canute built the church and inside, suspended from the roof, is a model of a Viking ship as a memorial to the Saxons and Danes who died at the Battle of Ashingdon (Assendun) in 1016.

The church is on a high hill looking across the green fields at the yachts on the River Crouch. A thousand years ago a Danish fleet was lying in the Crouch to take a defeated army back to Denmark.

The Saxon army led by King Edmund Ironside charged down Ashingdon hill on the retreating Danes under Canute. The Danes, faced with annihilation, turned and fought with the desperation of hopelessness.

Part of the Saxon army deserted and the battle raged all day to end in a disastrous defeat for the Saxons. The Danes soon controlled England and Canute was King.

Canute the Dane conquers Edmund Ironside and England

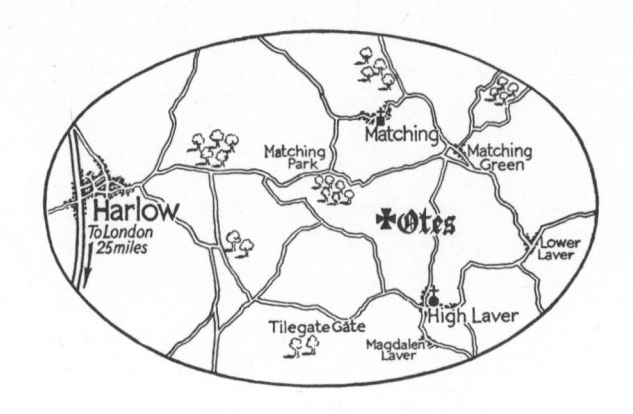

John Locke

A GREAT ENGLISHMAN

It is in High Laver churchyard that one of the greatest of Englishmen, John Locke, who was born in 1632 and died at the age of 72, lies buried. His grave is against the wall to the right of the porch and a bronze tablet has been erected to his memory.

Locke was the most brilliant man of his age. He studied medicine and became a distinguished doctor; he was also a Greek scholar, scientist, philosopher, economist and politician. Even the mighty Voltaire regarded Locke as his inspriation, and the present American constitution is based on his political ideas. He was also beyond question the father of English philosophy.

When he was 50 he met Damaris Cudworth then 24 and a brilliant young woman. She proposed marriage to him, but he told her he preferred her as a friend. Soon he was in love with her, but then she told him that her feelings had changed and he could only be her friend.

Sir Francis Masham was a country gentleman without any intellectual pretensions. At night Locke would join Lady Masham and her friends in the most brilliant intellectual circle of the time. Everybody came to Otes.

John Locke, who inspired Voltaire

One of Locke's friends was Sir Isaac Newton, who was often seen at High Laver. In 1693 Newton wrote an angry letter to Locke: *'Being of the opinion that you endeavoured to embroil me with women, I was so much affected with it as that when one told me you were sickly, I answered 'twere better if you were dead.'*

But they were soon friends again.

Locke occupied an important position in King William's government for some years, but in 1700 he retired owing to failing health. In 1703 he warned his friends that he would soon be dead, and the next year he died peacefully while Lady Masham was reading to him from the Psalms.

Not far away from the grave of John Locke is the grave of the famous Lady Abigail Masham, probably better known as Mrs. Masham, the woman who supplanted the formidable Duchess of Marlborough (Viceroy Sarah) at the court of Queen Anne.

It was the Duchess herself who introduced her cousin Abigail Hill to Queen Anne. Abigail set out to undermine the Duchess, and before long was the most influential person at Court. In 1707 she married Samuel Masham, a great grandson of the Sir Francis mentioned above, and remained the power behind the throne until Queen Anne died in 1714.

So great was her influence that her intrigues brought about the fall of one government, and she even plotted (unsuccessfully) to restore the Stuarts to the throne. In face of aristocratic opposition, Abigail had her husband made Baron Masham.

Retiring to High Laver Lady Masham died in 1734. Her grave may be seen in the churchyard among the Masham tombs at the back of the altar.

Locke's residence at Otes, near Harlow

Pleshey

TOWN OF EARTHWORKS

'*I SHOULD to Pleshey too*' . . . These words of the Duke of York in Shakespeare's '*Richard II*' should encourage us to visit the village of Pleshey, about seven miles north-west of Chelmsford.

An Eastern National bus from Ilford to Chelmsford, and another Eastern National bus to Pleshey, left me with the greater part of the day for wandering round a village which had been fortified by the Saxons against rhe Danes, and by an earlier people against the dangers of another invader.

Pleshey was the name given to the village by the Normans, and earlier, we are told, it was known as Tumblestoun, or the town of the tunnels or earthworks.

> . . . '*No massy door*
> *Grates on harsh hinges o'er the ruin'd floor;*
> *No pointed arch, with dread portcullis hung,*
> *Bids horror stalk the timid hinds among;*
> *No deep dark dungeon strikes their souls with fear,*
> *Nor swelling towers their threat'ning turrets rear,*
> *Yet still remains, and marks the ancient bound,*
> *The bold abutment of the outer mound;*
> *Still with a slow and pausing step we tread*
> *High o'er the lofty arch, and hence are led*

overleaf: four engravings of the Keep of Pleshey Castle

South

North

West

East

An Effigy said to represent Geoffrey de Mandeville, first Earl of Essex, formerly in the Temple Church, London, destroyed during World War II

PLESHEY

To mount the keep, whose hard access of yore
A moat defended – but defends no more;
For where of old did guardian waters flow,
Now spreading ash and humbler alders grow.'

All that is left of the once great castle at Pleshey are a huge mound approached by a brick bridge, the banks of the inner and outer baileys, and a moat round part of the inner bailey.

Geoffrey de Mandeville, the grandson of the de Mandeville who came over with William the Conqueror, held Pleshey castle among others, and was made Earl of Essex by King Stephen in 1141 in gratitude for the support given against Empress Matilda.

When the civil war turned in Matilda's favour, de Mandeville went over to her, and when the fortunes of war passed back to Stephen, de Mandeville went back to the King, who, however had him arrested and deprived him of his castles and his offices.

Pleshey castle passed to the de Bohuns through marriage, and afterwards to Thomas of Woodstock. Duke of Gloucester and uncle to Richard II and it was in 1397 that the Duke was enticed out of his castle by his nephew, Richard II on the pretext that his advice was needed in London on matters of state.

The King and the Duke rode through Epping Forest to Romford and then passed through Ilford. The Duke was kidnapped by Thomas Mowbray, Earl Marshal, soon after the party left Ilford by a lane leading to the River Thames.

This lane is believed to have been the present Green Street, or it may have been Katherine Road or High Street North, Manor Park.

Gloucester was taken to Calais where he was murdered.

The widowed Duchess of Gloucester retired in grief to Barking Abbey and Pleshey castle rapidly went to ruin. But the village, more ancient than the castle, remains and is one of our most delightful Essex villages beside the grim castle mounds which are a reminder of

'. . . old unhappy far off things.'

Dedham

FAMOUS ARTISTS

ANOTHER of the delightful old towns of Essex is Dedham on the River Stour. Once famous for its wool trade, it has many picturesque houses and the church was built about 1500 by one of the great wool merchants.

It seems impossible that this quiet little place in Essex was once the centre of a thriving industry which left behind as a memorial to the weavers the timbered Elizabethan houses and lovely church.

Dedham is on the edge of the Constable country. John Constable, one of the greatest of English painters, was born at East Bergholt in Suffolk in 1776 and died in 1837, and he said of the country round Dedham – *'These scenes made me a painter.'*

Constable came from a comfortably well-off middle-class country family. After a good education he was started in business by his father as a miller.

But John's inclinations were in another direction, and his father allowed him to go to London to study art.

He became so much the slave of his genius that it is said on one occasion he was so intent on his work in the open air that his body was absolutely still and a field mouse settled down in one of his pockets.

In the Victoria and Albert Museum are his pictures *Dedham Vale, Dedham Church,* the *'Cottage in a Cornfield'* and *Trees and Water on the Stour.* Not far from Dedham is the famous Flatford Mill. Other famous Essex pictures by Constable are *Hadleigh Castle and the Cornfield* (National Gallery) and *Harwich and Sea and Lighthouse* (Tate Gallery).

These pictures breathe the spirit of England 150 years ago – the fields, the water

The village of Dedham as Constable might have known it

mills, the river and the villages, of which he said he loved *'every stile and stump and every lane in the village, so deep rooted are early impressions.'*

Another painter who made his home at Dedham was Sir Alfred Munnings, who died at the age of 80 on 17th July 1959. Passionately hating what is known as *'modern art,'* he told with relish his famous story of Sir Winston Churchill:

'Alfred,' said Sir Winston, *'If we saw Picasso coming down this street towards us, would you join me in kicking a certain part of him?'*

'By God, Winston I would.' I recently read the three volumes of Munnings' Autobiography, and learned with surprise of his early work painting posters for Caley's Crackers and Waverley cycles.

One does not usually associate Sir Alfred Munnings with commercial art, but more with horses of all kinds – standing still, posing self-consciously, trotting and racing.

He painted gypsies and horse dealers besides Masters of Foxhounds and wealthy people, and there is something very special about his pictures, a vanished England, but still England.

For the greatest part of his life he was blind in one eye. He told the story of the accident with characteristic brevity. He was out with a greyhound, a sheepdog and a hound puppy. The two dogs passed through a hedge and as he lifted the puppy over a spray of thorn struck his right eye.

'*Sharp pain followed the blow. This was no mere flick against the eyeball. Soon I knew the worst. Standing among the swedes and shutting my left eye I saw nothing but grey fog.*'

Sir Alfred Munnings may not have been a great artist, but I think advice to art students would be echoed by many of us who have been puzzled by some meaningless intricate design and splash of colour.

'*If you paint a tree – for God's sake try and make it look like a tree, and if you paint a sky, try and make it look like a sky.*'

He was a great character and painted joyously the things he loved. When he wrote his biography, his comment in verse was:

> *Here in my preface let me state,*
>   *It is no use pretending*
> *That writing is an easy task –*
>   *That anyone can do it!*
> *It needs a well filled brandy flask*
>   *To help a fellow through it.*

And so, when we walk round Dedham let us remember two English artists who painted what they saw, without any nonsense, and do not need any art interpreters to explain the artist's message.

The Tudor Palace

AT BOREHAM

FOUR MILES from Chelmsford on the Colchester Road is the village of Boreham, which is famous for the Tudor palace, New Hall.

Walhfare in Boreham, granted by Earl Harold to his new college of secular canons about the year 1060, later formed part of New Hall, which has been connected through the centuries with many famous men and women of English history.

King John stayed at New Hall, and in 1347 Queen Philippa was received royally by the Lord Abbot of Waltham.

The Canons of Waltham Abbey exchanged New Hall for two smaller manors nearer the Abbey, and it was subsequently seized by Edward IV during the Wars of the Roses. Henry VII gave it to the Earl of Ormond as a reward for assistance during the revolution against Richard III and it afterwards passed to the Boleyns.

From Sir Thomas Boleyn it went to Henry VIII, and over the gateway may be seen Henry's coat of arms. Henry liked New Hall so much that he called it *Beaulieu* or *the beautiful place.*

The King often visited New Hall with various of his queens and Anne Boleyn gave a ball there to celebrate the birth of her daughter Elizabeth.

Henry's other daughter Mary, spent two unhappy years at New Hall when she was declared illegitimate after the King's marriage with Katharine of Aragon had been declared null and void.

Queen Elizabeth spent a month at New Hall with the Earl of Leicester in 1559, and it was sold in 1622 to George Villiers, Duke of Buckingham, for £30,000.

George Villiers was born in 1592 and was a good looking youth. At court he soon caught the eye of James I, and was made cupbearer. It was said of Villiers, *'He had neither political principles nor political alliances and for the time all he asked was to sun himself in the King's favour.'*

In 1616 he was made Viscount and the next year Earl. Two years later he was Marquis of Buckingham and Lord High Admiral.

During the first years of the reign of Charles I, he was caught up in the constitutional struggle between King and Parliament, and became more and more unpopular.

New Hall, the Tudor Palace at Boreham

The Duke had a presentiment that he would meet with a violent end and was assassinated at Portsmouth by a discharged soldier, John Felton, in 1628.

The second Duke of Buckingham was a Royalist in the Civil War, and the estate was seized by Parliament. Oliver Cromwell bought New Hall for five shillings, which it is said he sent contemptuously to the exiled Duke.

Reaney in his *History of Essex*, writes that Cromwell lived at New Hall for some time, although his official residence was at Hampton Court.

The Duke of Buckingham was reinstated after the Restoration but sold New Hall to General George Monk, Duke of Albemarle.

Charles II visited New Hall on a number of occasions and Nell Gwynne took part in a performance of '*The Merry Wives of Windsor*' in the Hall.

The last royal visitor was James II in May, 1686.

After a succession of owners, New Hall was purchased by an order of nuns, the Canonesses Regular of the Holy Sepulchre, in 1798, and it remains in their possession and occupation today.

Charles Dickens

AT CHIGWELL

WHICH was the Maypole described by Dickens? From the description in the first chapter of Barnaby Rudge it would appear to be the King's Head at Chigwell Village, but its position points to Chigwell Row.

Let Dickens speak for himself:

> 'The fact is, I patched it. The place in my mind was Chigwell Row, but I moved the "Kings Head" Inn to the site of the real "Maypole" as more suitable to my story.'

> '... an old building, with more gable ends than a lazy man would care to count on a sunny day.'

In the old days horse coaches used to run from the King's Head to Aldgate and also to the Maypole at Chigwell Row. When Ilford Railway Station was first built a coach ran regularly from the Maypole to Ilford. This is how the road to Ilford was described in Barnaby Rudge:

> '... had been ploughed up by the wheels of heavy wagons and rendered rotten by the frosts and thaws of the preceding winter, or possibly of many winters. Great holes and gaps had been worn into the soil; which being now filled with water from the late rains, were not easily distinguishable even by day.'

Barnaby Rudge begins and ends at the Maypole. Dickens gives his readers THE LOT. The story opens on a wild night and all comfortably before the fire in the inn, with a mysterious sinister stranger, and the story of a murder committed many years before.

The Maypole Inn, from Barnaby Rudge /by George Cruikshank

    The stranger, of course, is the murderer, and makes dramatic reappearances. There is the fire and terror of the Gordon Riots, villainous plotting, sacred and profane love and enough plots to give four or five novels a good start today.

    Lord George Gordon, John and Joe Willet, Dolly Varden, Solomon Daisy, Simon Tappertit and Barnaby Rudge with Grip, his raven are only a few of the immortal characters who belong to Chigwell Row.

    '*Chigwell my dear fellow*' wrote Dickens, '*is the greatest place in the world. Name your day for going. Such a delicious inn opposite the churchyard – such a lovely ride – such beautiful forest scenery – such an out-of-the-way rural place – such a sexton.*'

John Thurloe, secretary to Cromwell

The Rodings

AND JOHN THURLOE

BETWEEN Ongar and Dunmow is that part of Essex known as The Rodings or Roothings. The Rodings are all typical Essex villages as old as time.

Beauchamp Roding, Abbess Roding, Leaden Roding, Aythorpe Roding, High Roding, Margaret Roding, Berners Roding and White Roding like a family of ancients who will be dreaming away in Essex when the human race is settling in new towns on the Moon and Planets.

The village church of Beauchamp Roding is early Norman, but probably goes back to Saxon times. Abbess Roding in 1724 was described by Daniel Defoe as *'famous for good land, good malt and dirty roads; the latter indeed in the winter are scarce passable for horse or man.'*

It was called *'Abbess'* as it was originally one of the manors in the possession of Barking Abbey, and two famous men of the Civil War/Commonwealth period came from this small village.

Rookwood Hall was the home of the Capels, and Baron Capel was one of the Royalist garrison at Colchester in the siege of 1648, and was executed after the surrender of the city.

The other famous Abbess Roding man was John Thurloe, who became the right hand man of Oliver Cromwell.

He was born in 1616, the son of Thomas Thurloe, Rector of Abbess Roding, and specialised in the study of law, John Thurloe took no part in the Civil War, but established a great reputation at Lincolns Inn.

John Thurloe's name appears officially in December, 1652, as clerk to the committee for foreign affairs, from which his income was raised to £600, as he was already acting as secretary to the Council of State.

Rising rapidly to power and influence he signed the letters sent out to the sheriffs ordering them to proclaim Oliver Cromwell Lord Protector. Thurloe must have been the most powerful man in England, as in 1655 he was in charge of the intelligence department and in control of inland and foreign posts.

Never before or since has England had such an efficient secret service or diplomatic system. Cromwell was kept immediately informed of the plans of foreign powers and Thurloe's political police made certain that no plots or conspiracies had any chance of success.

Thurloe had spies at the exiled court of King Charles II, and it is said that Cromwell could tell royalists returning from abroad what had been said to them at secret interviews with King Charles II a few days before. *'Cromwell trusted none but his secretary Thurloe and sometimes not even him.'*

When Charles II returned to England in 1660. Thurloe was accused of treason, but within a month was freed, and agreed to be available for state service when required.

The arrest of Thurloe must have frightened many Royalists, as he said that in his secret records he had sufficient evidence to send many of the King's supporters to the scaffold, but nothing was revealed.

When England's reputation was at its lowest ebb under Charles II and the Dutch sailed into the Thames to destroy the British fleet, the Government were contemptuously reminded of the great Thurloe when *'Cromwell carried the secrets of all the princes of Europe at his girdle.'*

Thurloe was faithful to his old master and never returned to politics, although it was rumoured that Charles II invited him to advise on foreign affairs.

As far as it was known all Thurloe's secrets died with him, but many years later when William of Orange was King of England, a false ceiling was discovered in Thurloes' old chambers at Lincolns Inn. In this hiding place were the secret despatches, dossiers and papers of the Protectorate.

Many pleasant hours can be spent exploring the Rodings, and Aythorpe Roding has a noble survival of the past – a noble windmill, which looks as if it could grind all the corn of the Rodings.

Ongar

A MOST PLEASANT WALK

We leave the picturesque old town of Ongar by the Abridge and Romford road. At Marden Ash the road turns left for Brentwood and after another ¼ mile left again for Stondon Massey.

Crossing the River Roding at Hallsford Bridge, we soon arrive at Stondon Massey Church on the left of the road. Eight hundred years old, it is a typical Essex church with weather boarded bell tower and slender spire.

Not far from here at Stondon Place, William Byrd and his family lived for 30 years, Byrd has been described as the Father of Music and his pupil. Thomas Morley, said William Byrd was *'never to be named without reverence.'*

It was not until 1920, however, when it was possible to publish all his work that it was realised he was one of our greatest musical composers.

William Byrd was a Roman Catholic in an age of persecution by Protestants under Queen Elizabeth I, and was often in trouble for his religious views.

Passing over gentle hills, we see the Essex Weald at its best. Arriving in half a mile at the crossroads, we go straight on to Doddinghurst, a delightful old village. Keeping left at the next two road junctions, we soon see Blackmore Church with its red roof and white spire. Soon we are in Blackmore by Jericho Priory. This was often visited by Henry VIII, and it was said at court that he had gone to Jericho!

The moat of Ongar Castle a

stle House in about 1832

Ingatestone Hall, the home of Lord Petre

Retracing our steps for three-quarters of a mile, we turn left along a road signposted for Ingatestone.

The next mile by Fryerning Wood to Fryerning Church is my favourite Essex mile on a sunny afternoon. Three thousand years ago Bronze Age men lived at Fryerning, and there are traces of ancient burial mounds or barrows. As one would expect at such a village there are legends of ghosts and underground passages from Furze Hall up to Bedemans Berg in High Wood.

And it was near here that I passed a field with an unusual notice:

PRIVATE
PERSONS ENTERING
DO SO AT THEIR OWN
RISK.

Passing Fryerning Church, we turn right at the Woolpack with three-quarters of a mile to Ingatestone.

The disaster of 1897 is still remembered by many old people round Ingatestone. About 2.30 p.m. on 24th June the town was wrecked by a violent gale and hailstorm which swept across Essex.

Trees and chimney stacks fell like skittles, roofs were stripped of tiles, fences were blown down and carts overturned. The hail massacred hundreds of chickens and brought birds down from trees as if they had been shot.

So great was the damage that a subscription list was opened to assist all who had suffered in the storm.

The finest local house in Ingatestone Hall, which is still the home of Lord Petre, and is a Tudor manor house built between 1540 and 1565.

Part of the monument to the first Lord Petre, died 1613, and his wife Mary (Waldegrave) died 1604

Clavering

THE MOAT HOUSE MURDER

CLAVERING is an Essex village on the Hertfordshire border between Newport and Buntingford. The nearest railway station is Newport, on the Eastern line, and it is a three-mile walk to the village, which has an interesting church and many lovely old cottages.

It seems difficult to realise that 80 years ago this village was the scene of a sensational murder investigation, which made press headlines for weeks and became known as the Moat House murder.

Samuel Herbert Dougal lived at Moat House and was a popular man in the district. He was a genial sportsman, free with his money and owned one of the first motor cars in north west Essex.

There was much scandalous gossip about his love affairs, and stories that naked girls had been riding bicycles in one of his fields. There is an entry in his diary on 30 September 1902 – *'An extraordinary incident was witnessed by me tonight!'*

In the meantime, he had drawn all the money out of his bank accounts, but foolishly tried to change a £10 note in the Bank of England. This banknote had already been stopped in an effort to trace him, and Dougal was arrested for forgery.

As he and Detective Inspector Cox were walking along Cheapside, he bolted, but was unlucky enough to run into a cul-de-sac and was recaptured.

It was now clear that Miss Holland must be dead, probably murdered by Dougal, and for weeks the Moat House was searched, the garden dug to a depth of six feet, and the moat dragged and probed.

The police were about to give up when a labourer remembered that there had once been a drainage ditch. The man who had filled in the ditch four years before was brought to the farm and, from the information he gave, the police recommenced their digging.

A woman's body was found, which was identified as Miss Holland's by the clothing. The cause of death was obvious as there were two holes in the skull, one of which had a trace of lead on the edge and Dougal was charged with the wilful murder of Camille Holland by shooting her.

In 1898, Miss Camille Cecile Holland was 56-years-old and still very attractive. She was an intelligent and happy woman with a number of men friends. Her only love affair had been with a young naval officer in her youth. It had never come to anything as he had been drowned and, as a keepsake, his parents sent her his cornelian ring, which she always wore.

Samuel Herbert Dougal came into her life at a time when she needed an emotional friendship and, although very suspicious of his interest in her invested capital of £6,000-£7,000, she agreed to live with him. Dougal already had a wife, so he was not risking bigamy.

He had served 21 years 17 days in the army without losing a day for bad conduct, but there was a long record of seduced girls, who had parted with their money and been abandoned. There were also two wives of his who had died mysteriously after short and painful illnesses!

Dougal had appeared in court twice on criminal charges – the first being for arson, when he was acquitted, and the second for forgery when he received a sentence of 12 months hard labour and lost his army pension.

It was when he was practically destitute and past 50 that he met the well-to-do spinster of 56 – Miss Holland.

After living together for some months at Saffron Walden, they moved to Coldhams farm (Moat House) on 27 April, 1899.

Needless to say with a man of Dougal's temperament there was trouble with the young servants, and Miss Holland reproached him for his behaviour.

On Friday, 19 May, the two went shopping and Miss Holland was never seen alive again. Within a few days of her murder Dougal was forging cheques on her accounts and selling her investments. It seems probable that if he had quietly disappeared with Miss Holland's money the murder would never have been discovered and he would have lived in comfort for the rest of his life.

Dougal came up for trial at Chelmsford on 22 June, 1903, and was sentenced to death the next day. He was hanged on 14 July.

Billericay

ONCE THE CAPITAL OF ESSEX

Long before the Romans civilised England there was a village or settlement at Billericay. The Romans came to Billericay and after a few centuries vanished beneath the rush of Saxon invaders.

Billericay (or the neighbouring Great Burstead) is said to have been the capital of the Kingdom of Essex 1300 years ago, with King Sebert or Sigeberht having a great house there.

Even its name is wrapped in mystery, as none of the wise and learned men of today can offer any suggestion on its origin.

This little Essex town has been the scene of three great dramas during the last 600 years.

At the end of the Great Revolt in 1381, the Essex men made their last stand in the forest north of the town. Behind primitive defences of old farm carts, they were no match for the armoured horsemen of Thomas of Woodstock, uncle of King Richard II, who slaughtered the labourers like sheep.

It is believed that the dead were buried in the churchyard of Great Burstead.

There must be something indomitable about the people of Billericay, as when the persecution of the Protestants started during the reign of Queen Mary, not only men and women, but boys and girls, went cheerfully to die at the stake at Chelmsford, Stratford and Newgate.

Sixty years later four people from Billericay went on one of the greatest adventures of all time – they joined the Pilgrim Fathers on the voyage of the *Mayflower.*

In 1620 Christopher and Marie Martin, Solomon Prower and John Langerman left Billericay to escape religious intolerance, said goodbye to their native land and left Plymouth for the New World.

Tragedy overtook the small party from Billericay, as they died on the *Mayflower* while she was off the coast of Massachusetts. Here is a description of the beginnings of the Pilgrims' settlement:

'Despite a severe winter during which more than half the inhabitants died, the colony survived, and most of its members were soon making an adequate living from the fur trade, farming, fishing and lumbering.'

But men and women left Essex towns and villages in search of religious freedom, and there is a Billericay in U.S.A., as also a Chelmsford and a Braintree and many other Essex place names.

Three hundred years later a German Zeppelin was shot down in flames close by Billericay, and the men who perished were buried in Great Burstead Churchyard beside the ancient King of Essex and the nameless country folk who died in the Great Revolt of 1381.

In the words of Arthur Mee's *'Essex'* *'To walk down the High Street is like walking through 400 years.'*

Times have changed and Billericay is now part of Basildon.

The Riches

OF FELSTED

IN THE PLAY '*A Man For All Seasons*' at the Globe Theatre, there is an ignoble and unscrupulous man, Richard Riche, who was responsible for the condemnation and sentence of death on Sir Thomas More.

Richard Riche was destined to found an important Essex family, became Lord Riche before he died, and founded Felsted School. His descendants rose still higher, and the Riches became Earls of Warwick.

In the Riche chapel in Felsted church, Richard Riche's tomb is on the south wall, and a venerable Elizabethan statesman, with a long beard, leans wearily on his left elbow and looks sadly and thoughtfully into the future.

Richard Riche was a successful lawyer who was at first Member of Parliament for Colchester and afterwards for Essex. In 1533 Lord Chancellor Thomas Audley made him Solicitor-General, and in 1536 he was Speaker of the House of Commons. At the same time he received extensive grants of land from Henry VIII in the Felsted area. He was of great assistance to the government when the dissolution of the monasteries took place, and was the head of the office dealing with the spoils from the religious houses.

Richard Riche

Riche was a true '*Vicar of Bray*', as he changed his loyalties and religion whenever it suited his interests.

When Edward VI died in 1553, he declared first for Lady Jane Grey, but transferred to Mary when the Earl of Oxford joined her. Riche entertained Queen Mary at Wanstead House, and declared for Queen Elizabeth when she came to the throne.

He acted at the great state trials of Henry VIII reign and was instrumental in sending many great men to the scaffold. In Mary's reign he sent Protestants to the stake, and during Elizabeth's reign Roman Catholics were his victims.

He founded Felsted School on 21st May, 1564, and this school became one of the most famous in Essex.

As Lord Riche he died at Rochford Hall and there was a great funeral procession to convey his body to Felsted church.

The second Lord Riche bought the title of Earl of Warwick from James I for £18,000. There were only four Earls of Warwick with the name Riche, as a series of deaths caused the Earldom to pass to the Earl of Holland.

Probably the most famous boys who went to Felsted School were the Cromwells. It has been suggested that the Lord Protector Oliver Cromwell was once a student, but there is nothing to support this opinion.

The Lord Protector's four sons went to Felsted. The eldest son Robert died at Felsted at the age of 18, and was buried there. The second son Oliver died of smallpox in 1644 while serving in his father's regiment.

The Lord Protector's successor, Richard Cromwell, was a Felsted old boy, but had no wish to inherit his father's greatness. Tumbledown Dick, as he was called, ended his days as an obscure country gentleman, and is remembered in the nursery rhyme.

> '*Hickory Dickory Dock,*
> *The mouse ran up the clock,*
> *The clock struck one,*
> *The mouse ran down;*
> *Hickory Dickory Dock.*'

The mouse was of course, poor Tumbledown Dick.

Oliver Cromwell, the Lord Protector

Braintree

AND BOCKING

BRAINTREE AND BOCKING are inseparable Essex towns. They have grown together, and in April, 1934, they were amalgamated into the Braintree and Bocking Urban District Council. Since 1974 they formed the heart of the Braintree District.

The *'Four-and-twenty'* governed Braintree from at least 1565. They were the leading citizens of Braintree and operated as a Select Vestry for parish business. In 1574 they were described as the Twenty-four Headboroughs, and later as the Governors of the Town and Town Magistrates.

The imposing parish church of St. Michaels was built in the thirteenth century, and is of particular interest to readers who are interested in the history of the theatre, as it is probable that English comedy was born at Braintree.

The church was considerably enlarged between 1522 and 1535 and to help towards the cost of these improvements three religious or *'mystery'* plays were acted in the church. These plays told the stories or legends of Saints – St. Swithin in 1523, St. Andrew in 1525 and St. Eustace in 1534.

The performances of these plays must have been great occasions at Braintree and generous arrangements were made for supplying the audiences with food and drink. *'These were not only for pleasing the eye and ear, but likewise for satisfying the belly; for which great provision was always made.'*

Unfortunately the churchwardens later (at the Reformation) sold the players' garments for 50/- (£2.50) and the playbooks for 20/- (£1.00). If these playbooks should be found they might be worth more than the earliest Shakespeare folio.

Nicholas Udall was vicar of Braintree from 1533 to 1537, and it is believed that he wrote the play of St. Eustace. Udall became headmaster of Eton in 1534 and headmaster of Westminster in 1553. He was a man of many gifts and the outstanding playwright of his time. Ralph Roister Doister, the first English comic play, was written by him and first performed by the boys of Westminster School in 1553, and was probably inspired by his experiences at Braintree.

Close by the church is a great fountain, the centre piece of which is a beautiful statue of a young man representing Youth. He seems to be springing into the air after all the ideals of youth.

Courtaulds was founded at Panfield Lane, Bocking, in 1816, and factories were soon established at Braintree, Bocking and Halstead. From 1906 rayon was woven, dyed and finished, and were 1,800 local people employed in the Essex mills: but these have now all closed.

The Courtaulds have been the benefactors of modern Braintree, and among their gifts are a library, hospital and nurses' home.

The other famous industry of Braintree is Crittall Ltd. Francis Crittall's mother injured herself trying to raise a heavy wooden-framed window, and her son set about inventing a light metal-framed window, which could be handled easily. This was over fifty years ago, but Crittall's dates back to 1635, and is the oldest ironmongery business in England.

In the old coaching days there were many old inns, but most of these have now gone and the old buildings have been transformed into shops and offices.

overleaf: A view of Braintree in the early nineteenth century

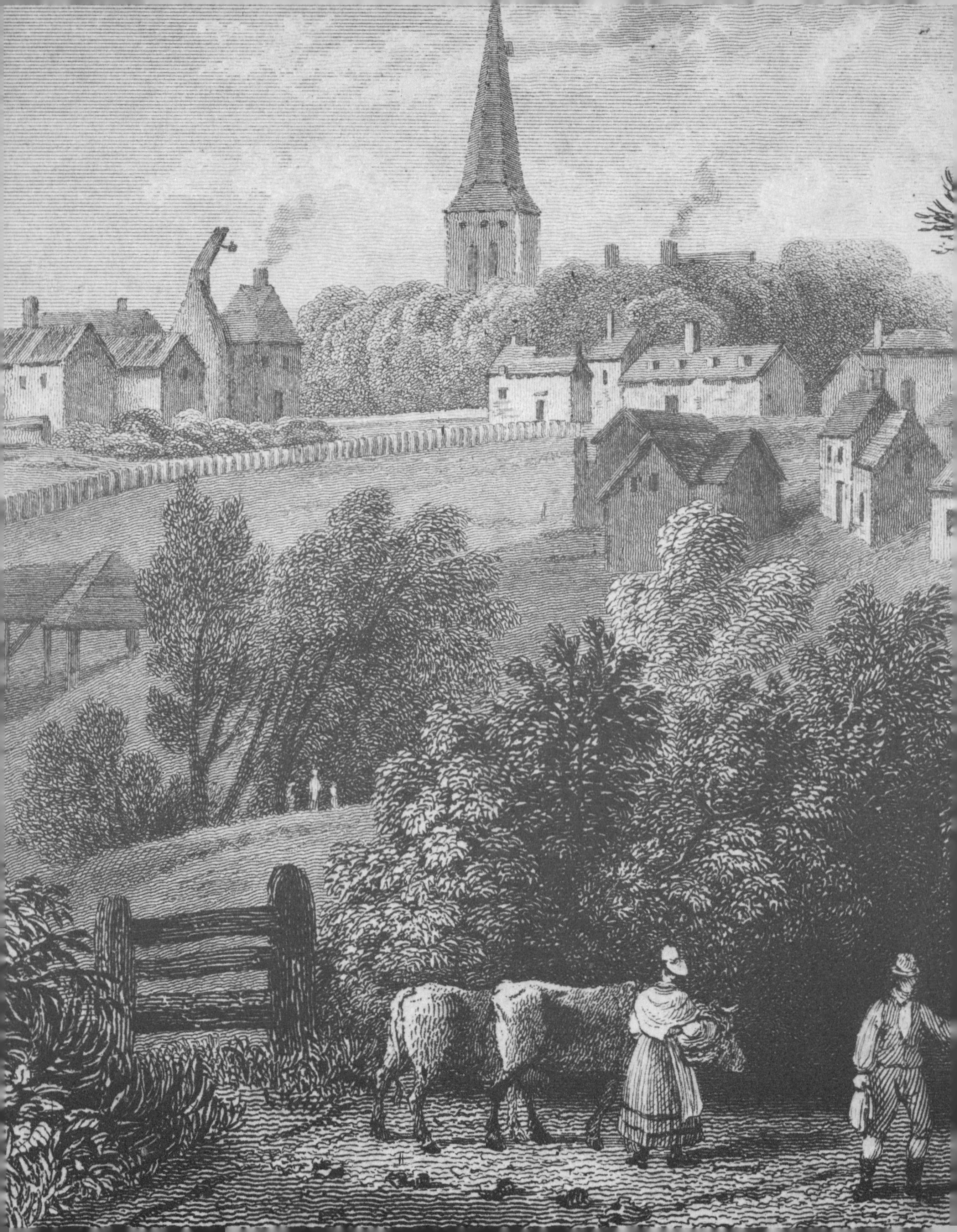

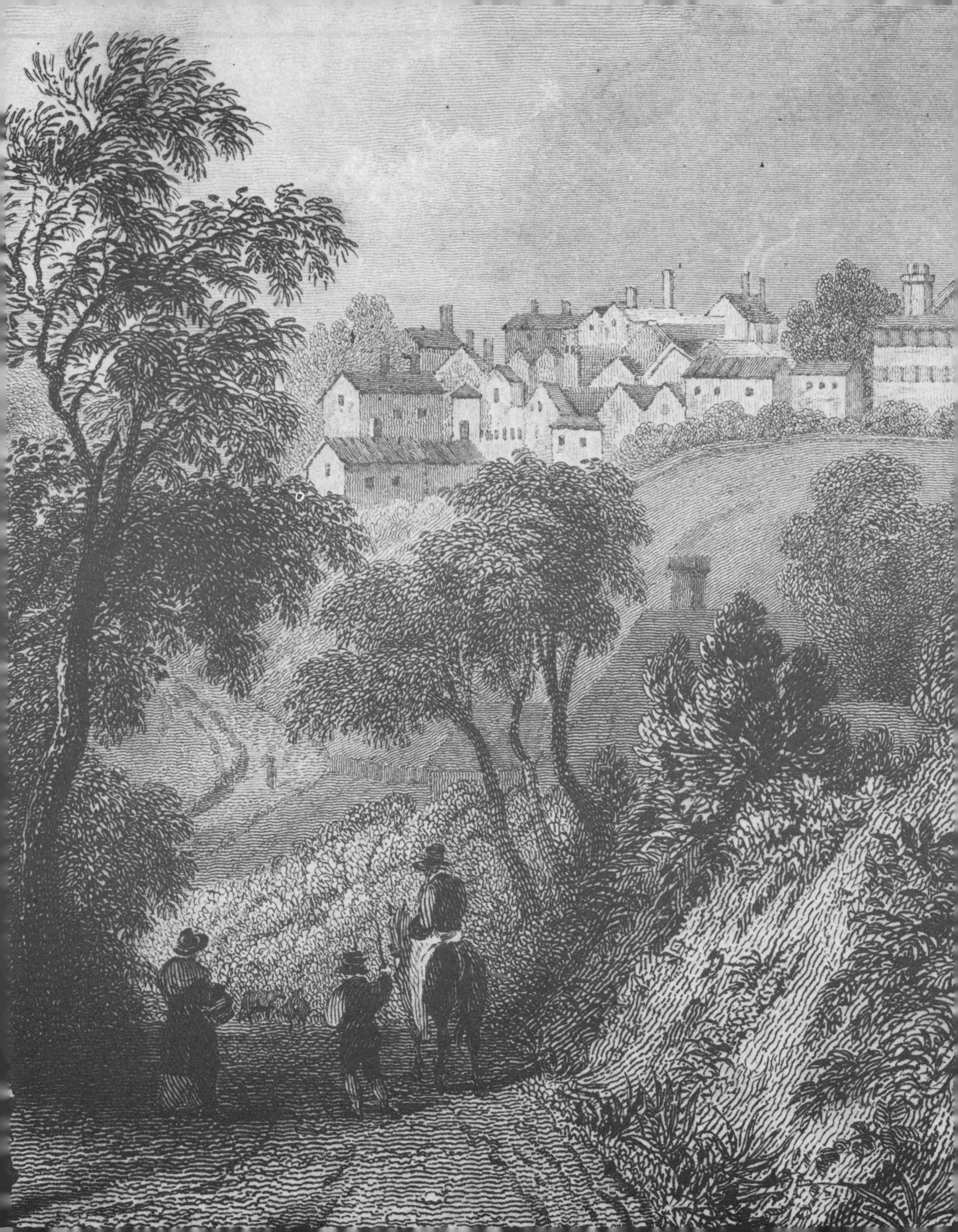

Tilty Abbey

AND THE HEADLESS MONK

Tilty Abbey of St. Mary's stood midway between Thaxted and Great Dunmow, one mile west of the present main road A130.

Tilty church was originally the gatehouse chapel and entrance to the Cistercian Abbey, which was founded about 1153. The church has been restored and is lovely and austere with some very beautiful brasses.

King John, plunderer of Tilty Abbey

In the church there is a plan of the old abbey, which was prosperous and rich in its early years.

When King John ravaged Essex, his soldiers broke into Tilty Abbey on Christmas Day 1215 when Mass was being celebrated. Mr. Francis Steer in '*A Short*

History of Tilty' is of the opinion that the monks resisted the soldiers and some were killed.

For centuries there has been a legend of a headless monk haunting the lanes, and when Mr. Steer excavated the site of the abbey in 1942 he found the grave of a skeleton without a skull. He considered that this was a monk who had been decapitated by the royal soldiers in 1215, and the legend of the ghost of the headless monk had survived in the village.

During the early part of the 14th century a large quantity of wool was sent from Tilty to wool merchants in Italy, and it was some bad debts that plunged the abbey into its financial difficulties, from which it never extricated itself.

Men from the abbey quarrelled over corn with men from St. John's Hospital at Broxted. In a fight which followed a number were wounded, and the St. John's men fled and were hotly pursued to Broxted by the men from Tilty.

The abbey's financial difficulties continued until its dissolution in 1536, when there were only the abbot, and five monks in residence.

Partial demolition took place and building material was carried away to the surrounding villages. There are gargoyles in the walls of houses near Thaxted which might have come from the abbey. Apart from Tilty church, the only other remains of the abbey are some fragments of the walls.

Leaving Tilty I made for Dunmow. After a mile I was stopped by a motorist who asked me the way to Tilty Abbey. He invited me to return to Tilty with him and then drive me on to Dunmow, I agreed and again inspected the church and the ruins.

My new friend in the car, who came from Braintree, mentioned that he was visiting all the abbeys in Essex and, on my mentioning Leighs Priory, immediately suggested that we should go there, which we did, and also visited the Black Chapel at North End near Felsted, but that is another story.

He drove me back to Great Dunmow, where I caught the bus to Chelmsford.

The Saffron Crocus

OF WALDEN

THE SAFFRON CROCUS was once grown extensively round Walden, so the town became Saffron Walden, and an ancient people lived there long before the Romans came to Essex. The Saxons called it Walden, which is believed to have meant the Valley of the Strangers.

There is a Saxon burial ground in the town, in the area known as Battle Ditches. This was excavated during the 19th century, and over 200 graves were revealed. The skeletons lay in tombs cut out of the solid chalk, and in Saffron Walden Museum it is possible to see the bones of our Saxon ancestors who lived and died in Walden over one thousand years ago.

There are many old inns in Saffron Walden, most of which are preserved as buildings of historic and architectural interest.

Saffron Walden in the early ninteenth century

At the corner of Market Hill and Church Street is one of the oldest buildings in the town. This was originally the Sun Inn, at which Oliver Cromwell and General Fairfax made their headquarters during the crisis of the Civil War 1646/7.

The army of King Charles had been destroyed, and Cromwell's New Model Army was reorganising at Saffron Walden.

Parliament began to fear its own army which, from being the servant of Parliament, was rapidly becoming its master.

The Army asked for arrears of pay, pensions for widows and dependants and some security for the future. Cromwell and Fairfax met the Commissioners of Parliament at the Sun Inn in a vain attempt to settle the Army's claims. So incensed did Parliament become that it was proposed to arrest Cromwell and other Army leaders.

In May, 1647, Parliament demanded that the New Model Army should be disbanded. Charles was now in a strong position, as Parliament needed his authority. Secret plans were laid for a concentration of military forces in London, and for a Scottish army to march down from the North.

At the critical moment Cromwell acted with speed and determination. The King was taken prisoner and the artillery at Oxford, which Parliament was going to use against the New Model Army, was seized. The New Model Army marched on London and Parliament capitulated.

The slight chance of a general settlement between King and Parliament was lost at Saffron Walden, and the Second Civil War of 1648 became inevitable.

Charles played his last card and a Royalist insurrection took place. Colchester was taken by the Cavaliers and a Scottish army invaded England. Cromwell routed the Scots at Preston and Colchester surrendered to Fairfax. King Charles was executed in Whitehall on 30th January 1649.

The builder of the first Eddystone Lighthouse came from near Saffron Walden. Henry Winstanley was born in 1644. He became clerk of works at Audley End which was then a royal palace.

He invented all kinds of strange devices, and when he was over 50 planned the first Eddystone Lighthouse off Plymouth. It was over 120 feet high and stood the strain of storms and wind until the great gale of 1703, which swept away the lighthouse with Winstanley inside it.

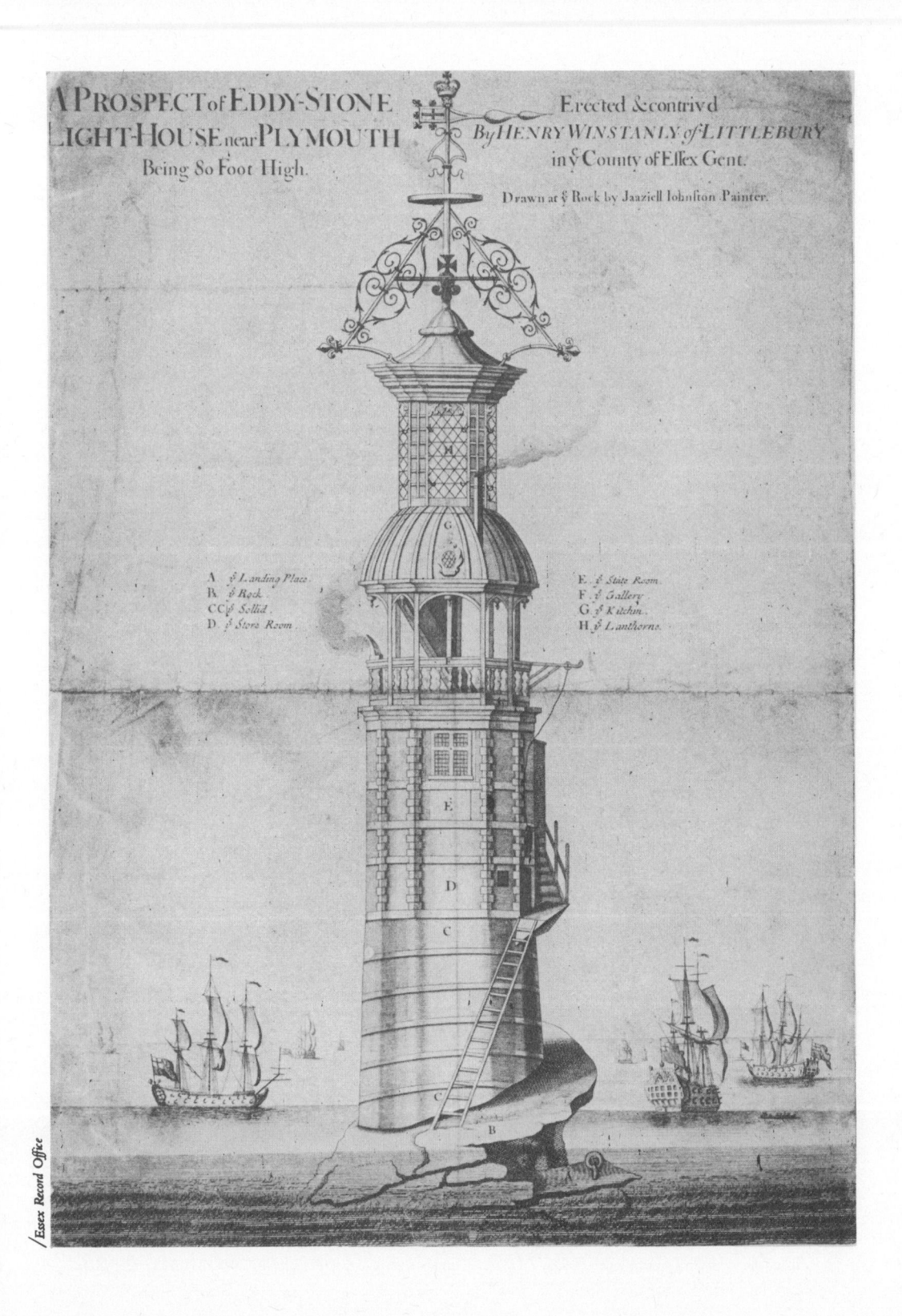

A PROSPECT of EDDY-STONE
LIGHT-HOUSE near PLYMOUTH
Being 80 Foot High.

Erected & contriv'd
By HENRY WINSTANLY of LITTLEBURY
in ye County of Essex Gent.

Drawn at ye Rock by Jaaziell Johnston Painter.

A ye Landing Place.
B ye Rock.
CC ye Sollid.
D ye Store Room.
E ye State Room.
F ye Gallery.
G ye Kitchin.
H ye Lanthorne.

Robert Fitzwalter

AND THE DUNMOW FLITCH

Dunmow immediately suggests the Dunmow Flitch, which originated in Little Dunmow, but this village has a claim to greater fame than the Flitch, as Robert Fitzwalter was Lord of Dunmow and Baynards Castle. There are many Fitzwalter tombs in Little Dunmow, but, although careful search has been made, that of Robert has never been found.

It was in 1215 that Robert Fitzwalter led the barons' army against King John, when London was seized and the King forced to sign Magna Carta at Runnymede. In Little Dunmow Church there is a tablet in memory of Robert Fitzwalter with the following inscription:

> FOUNDER OF OUR CIVIL LIBERTY
> MARSHALL OF THE ARMY
> OF GOD AND HIS CHURCH

There is a legend that his daughter, Matilda attracted the attention of King John. She resisted the King's advances and to escape him became a nun. John's desire for her grew stronger and, in his frustration, he had her poisoned.

Another legend of Little Dunmow is that Sir Reginald Fitzwalter started the custom of the Dunmow Flitch by swearing on oath that he and his wife had not had a difference of opinion in 12 months.

The prior gave them a flitch as a reward, and Sir Reginald then gave lands to the priory on condition that a flitch should be given to any couple who would swear on oath that they had not had a cross word for a whole year.

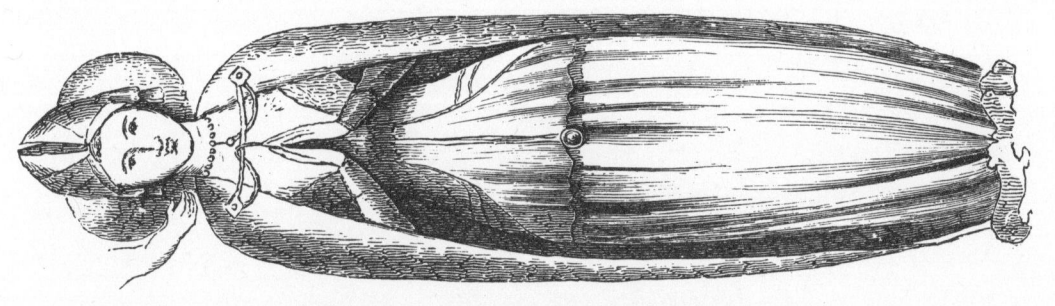

The effigy at Dunmow of Matilda Fitzwalter

But the custom of the flitch probably goes back long before the Fitzwalters to Saxon times, and bacon has been the reward of virtue in many parts of Europe. Francis Steer in *'The History of the Dunmow Flitch Ceremony'* quotes a local opinion: 'Them ancient foaks – maybe the Rumans – guv' a bit o'bacon to them as didn't whop their missus.'

The earliest mention of the Dunmow Flitch is in Chaucer, and the first record of a flitch being awarded was in 1445, when Richard Wright of Bawburgh, near Norwich, was awarded a flitch by the Prior of Dunmow.

The last public award by the lord of the manor was in 1741, when Thomas and Ann Shakeshaft took the oath:

> 'That you never made any Nuptial transgression
>   Since you were married man and wife
> By Household Brawls or Contentious Strife
>   Or otherwise in Bed or at Board
> Offended each other in Deed or in Word
>   Or since the Parish Clerk said Amen
> Wish'd yourself unmarri'd agen
>   Or in Twelve months and a day
> Repented not in thought in any way.'

The Shakeshafts got their bacon and were carried in procession in a chair which is still preserved in the church.

For 100 years the ceremony lapsed, until it was revived in 1855, when a trial for

overleaf: the Dunmow Flitch ceremony in 1751, published 1752/Rose Caunt

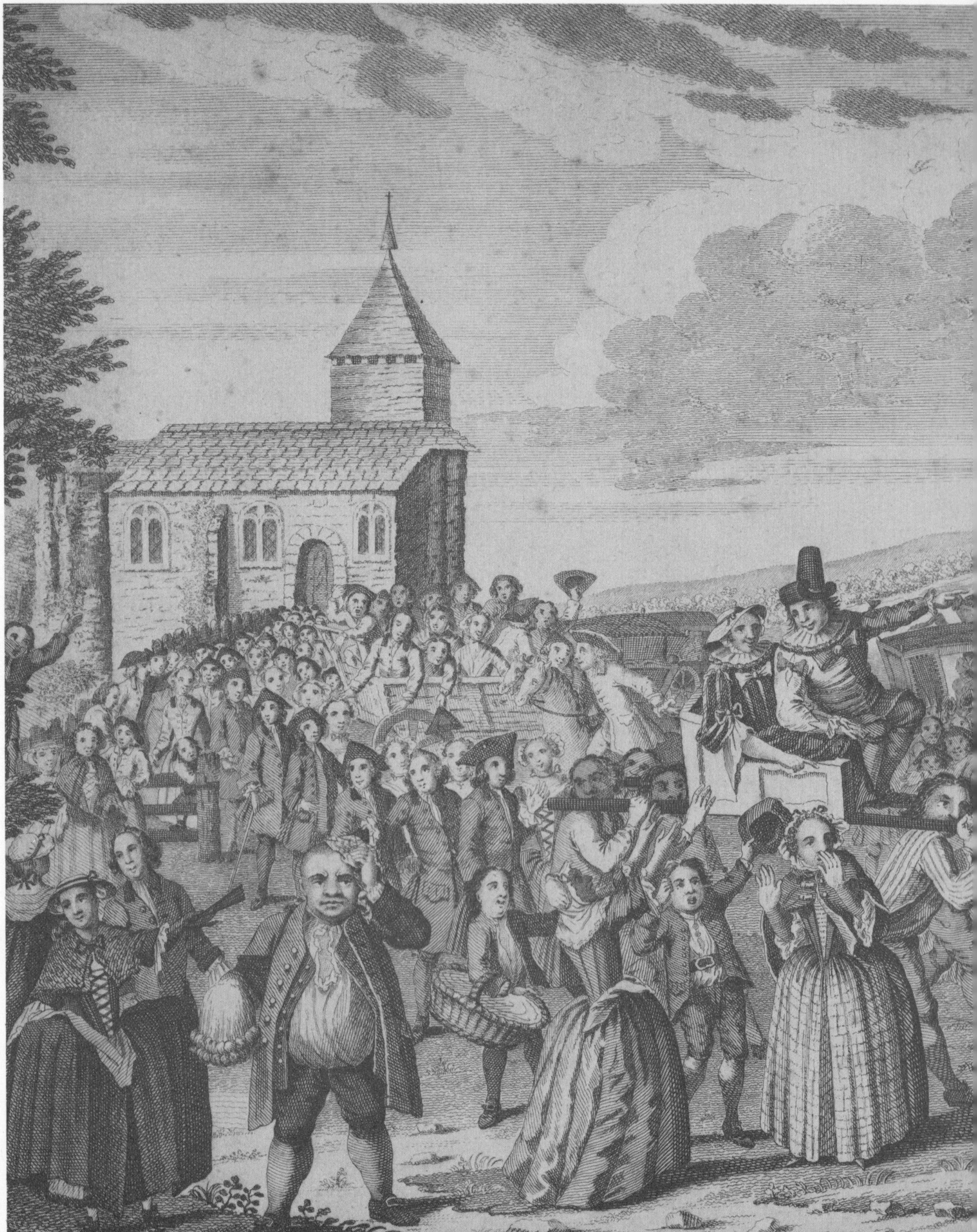

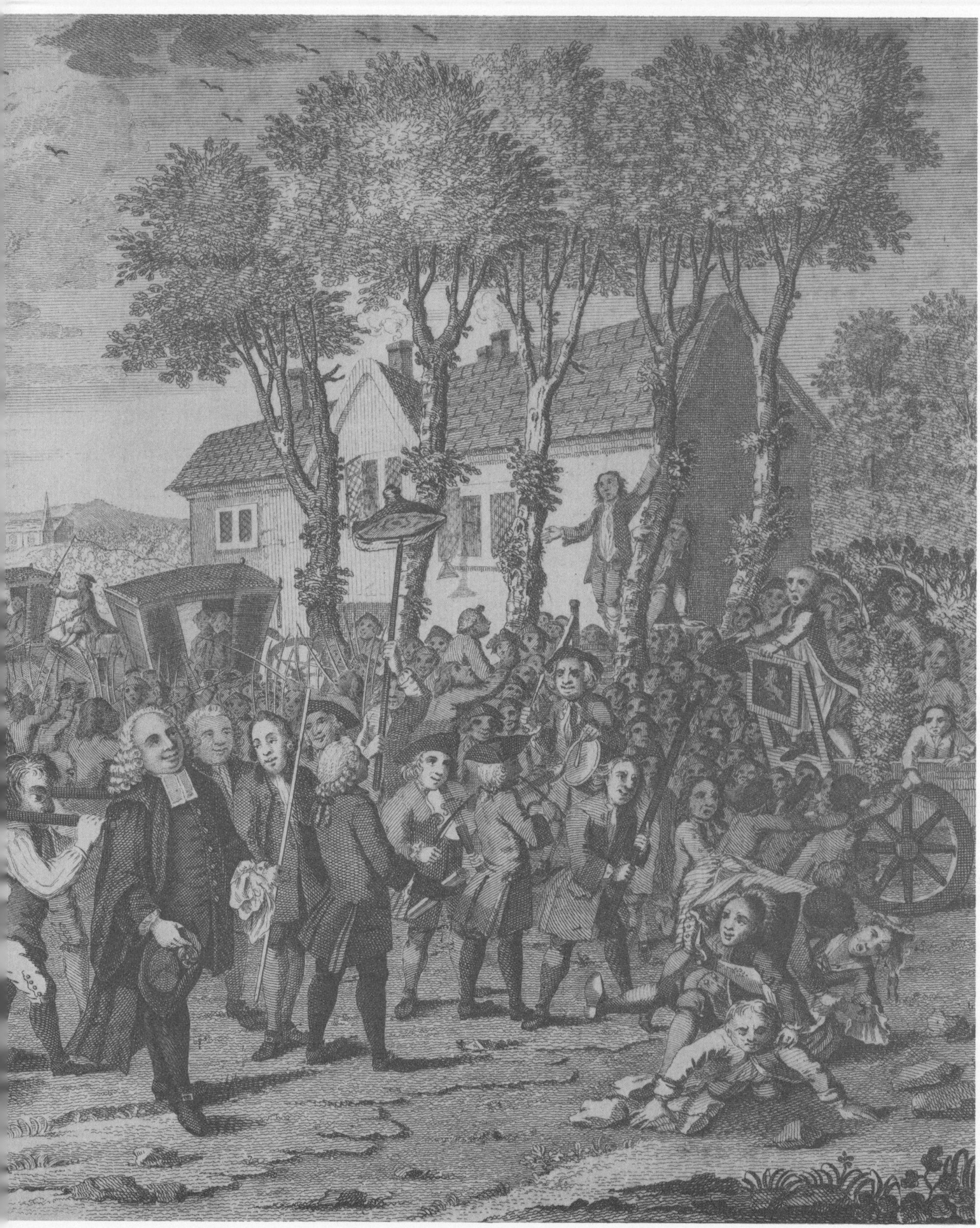

the flitch was held in the Town Hall at Great Dunmow. Two flitches were awarded before an audience estimated at 7,000.

Trials were held fairly regularly at Great Dunmow until World War I, and then Ilford stepped in with Dunmow Flitch trials in 1920, 1929, 1930 and 1932. Dunmow resented this impertinence from Ilford and, according to Francis Steer, one comment at Dunmow was:

'Oi down't reckon oi know where this ole Ilford plice is; oi count that must be somewhere out furrin, Ilford? Ne'er he'erd tell on't.'

Dunmow Flitch trials are now held all over England, perhaps the World, but it would seem that to keep to the spirit of the custom the bacon should come from Dunmow, and everyone knows that Essex bacon is as good as Wiltshire or Danish any day.

The examination of candidates for the Dunmow Flitch in the Town Hall at Great Dunmow

The Epping Hunt

IN THE ROYAL FOREST

Although Londoners still go to Epping Forest at Easter, Whitsun and August, these holidays are nothing like the great cockney riot of the Epping Hunt, which is believed to have started in 1226 and went on until the 1850's.

Tradition has it that Richard I *Coeur-de-Lion* (1189-1190) in return for certain services allowed the Lord Mayor and citizens to use the Royal forest of Epping to hunt the deer.

So, on Easter Monday from Cheapside to Stepney Green, thousands made for Buckhurst Hill and Chingford. On horse and donkey, in chaise, cart and waggon, cockneydom moved out en masse.

Tom Hood, an eye witness of the Hunt, wrote:

'*All sorts of vehicles and vans,*
Bad, middling and the smart;
Here rolled along the gay barouche,
And there a dirty cart.'

The horses were described in the *Sporting Review* as easy goers, and no goers, kickers and bolters, dancers and prancers, leapers and creepers, long-tailed, bob-tailed, rat-tailed and no-tailed.

The riders were dressed in all manner of coats and some had no coats at all, and were baronets, butchers, dandies, dustmen, knifegrinders, sweeps, members of the nobocracy and snobocracy.

The shouting multitude made for a part of the forest between High Beech and Chingford, known as Fairmead Bottom. Here were refreshment stalls, booths,

The Epping Hunt passes the Old Green Man/Rose Caunt

gambling tables and all the fun of the fair.

A great shout would go up when the hounds arrived, but in later years the hounds were a very miscellaneous collection of dogs borrowed from far and near.

The stag was brought up in a cart from one of the local inns, where it had been stabled. When it was turned out the poor beast was often dazed by the noise but soon set off at great speed.

Let Hood describe it:

> 'And now began a sudden stir.
> And then a sudden shout,
> The prison doors were opened wide
> And Robin bounded out.
> One curious gaze of wild amaze.

He turned and shortly took;
Then gently ran adown the mead
And bounded o'er the brook.'

The Hunt did not always end with the death of the stag, as some survived to be hunted year after year, and often made straight back to the paddock at Woodford. There is a story that one wily old deer turned left when he should have turned right. The Hunt turned right and blundered on through the forest chasing everything that came its way.

Tom D'Urfey in *'Pills to Purge Melancholy'* describes such a scene:

'My Lord Mayor takes a staff in hand to beat the bushes o'er,
I must confess it was hard work he ne'er had done before,
A creature bounded from the bush, which made them all to laugh,
My lord, he cried, "A hare! a hare!" but it proved an Essex calf.'

The scene in the forest must have been like a battlefield after a cavalry charge, with riderless horses trotting in all directions, hundreds of lost hats and men wearily trudging towards the nearest inn.

There was a happy ending to it all, as the gallant huntsmen arrived at such local inns as the Castle, Horse and Groom, Bald Faced Stag, Roe-Buck, Robin Hood and King's Oak, where magnificent dinners and suppers were washed down with bumpers of beer and wine. Trotting back to London many stories were told of astounding feats of horsemanship, and miraculous escapes from the dangers of the chase.

List of Subscribers

Mr S. Alexander
Anbrosia Books Ltd
Mrs G. Armstrong

E.M. Baker
J.A. Baker
Ann Banks
Mrs V.E. Banks
Mr & Mrs Edward C. Barber
Miss Anne E. Barker
Jean Barnet
Mrs E. Benians
Benjamin Bailey & Co.
Mr Alexander Bennewith
G. Bertram
Alfred A. Best
Bill and Mary Bird
Anthony Bispham
Trevor and Diana Bond
Ian Bonner
The Bookstack Limited
E. A. Brett
Dr. Michael E. Brett
Jennifer Ann Brewer
Len and Katie Brickwood
Briggs Art and Bookshop
Adrian Tancred Brooks
D. Brown
Browsers Bookshop
Anne Bruce
Harold Bruce
Mr & Mrs Ivan R. Buck
Burgess Bookshop

Mr & Mrs W.S. Burgess
James and Hilda Burnell
Mr and Mrs I.F. Burns
Mrs J. Byrne

Sarah Carolan
David Carter
The Castle Bookshop
Rose Caunt
R.T.S. Charlton
Rex Chartres
Chelmsford Borough Council;
    Chelmsford & Essex Museum
A.H.R. Christian
Colonel J.H. Clarke
J.H. Clarke & Co. Ltd
The Compass Bookshop
David M. Coombes
Heather Cooper
Miss M. Copsey
Sue and Dave Cowling
Graham Cox

Catherine R. Daniels

William H. Emery
Charles and Joan Erwood

Mary Frazer

H. Gearing
Barbara Gil-Rodriguez
Mr & Mrs D.M. Grounds

Benjamin Gunby
Selwyn Guy

Mrs J. Hammond
Hannay Booksellers
P.E. Hawke
J. Hayward
Heffers Booksellers
Stuart Henderson
Mr & Mrs Paul Hodge
George Hogarth
Elizabeth Holloway
Bari Hooper

W. Noel Jackson
F.A. & P.E. Jeff
Eileen M. Johnson
Terry Johnson
Enid M. Jones

J.P. Kelly
M.L. Kelly
J.W. King

S.E. Land
Martin and Gwen Levison
F.J. Levitt
Mr & Mrs L.A. Lewis
Dr. P.M. Lewis
Mr David G. and Mrs Julia R.
    Ling
Elisabeth Littlejohn

LIST OF SUBSCRIBERS

Mr P.J. Lovell
Mrs Edith Lynch

Mrs S.P. Masters
Mrs Doris Mattock
B. Mawhinney
Douglas B. May
Mr & Mrs John McIntosh

Patrick O'Conor
Mrs Micheal O'Hara
Olive Orchard

Philip B. and Anne B. Parker
Passmore Edwards Museum
Mr & Mrs K.L. Pearmain
Joe Pickett
Mike Pickett
The Pied Piper Bookshop
Mrs P. Pitt
Raymond Port

Redbridge Reference Library
Dr. May Reed

Miss Eileen Riches
Derek L. Riches
H.W. and L.A. Robbins

Mr J. Sage
Miss Eirene Sarfas
Daphne Elizabeth Scott
H.M. Seabrook
Leslie W. Sherman
Evelyn Kyle Thomas Shirley
Keith W. Sizer
Revd. William J.T. Smith
Shirley I. Smith
W.H. Smith & Son Ltd. Colchester
W.H. Smith & Son Ltd. Saffron Walden
Harry and Joan Stevens
Maria Szczypinska

Mr Hermon Taylor
Thomas & Pauline Thaw

James H. Thompson
C.H. Thomson

Harold G. Venus
Wynne D. Venus
Victoria and Albert Museum

R.J. Wager
J.A. Wall
Waltham Forest Public Libraries
Mr Francis W. Warren
Mr & Mrs O. Watts
Mary M. Webb
Gilbert A. White
Margaret and Andrew White
Alan E.A. Wild
Joyce Wilkie
David Wilkinson
Dr. and Mrs J.R.B. Williams
Mrs E.I.O. Willsmer
Hazel and Alan Wilson
Olga Ironside Wood
Mrs E.J. Woolmore

THE forest in winter, the forest in spring, in summer, and in autumn—which is finest? Indeed, I do not know. . . . Truly the forest is very magnificent in summer, when under the trees the brilliant light is held in check by the thick leafage. But for those who can see, there is a greater magnificence in late autumn. For then the woods lie over the hills in a broken tumult of mellow colour. All shades—brilliant yellow, full browns, sober crimsons, and heavy olives—mingle in a strange harmony, as sober and as quiet as it is rich. But then the winter brings beauties of its own. When the hoar-frost makes the woods a world of white lace, when the ground is like granite and the clear air is sharp and tingling on the face, you may stand in Monk Wood, or you may overlook the forest from Loughton Camp, and see that natural beauty is no mere matter of green leaves and golden sunlight. . . . And for the remaining season, have not a hundred poets sung of spring in the woods? When the sap rises over the six thousand acres of Epping Forest here is spring indeed, spring as no words can paint it. But for that—go and see.

ARTHUR MORRISON, *The Traveller*, July 1901.

REGR Wy
[Coll 27/3/17)
FIRST EDN
1983 vi + 122 pp.
Numerous dpl, f.p.
& other text sepia illusts
2 dpl f.p. c.p. maps
ASBy

The county of Essex by William Morgan, dedica